REGIONAL INTEGRATION
IN
WEST AFRICA

REGIONAL INTEGRATION IN WEST AFRICA

IS THERE A ROLE FOR A SINGLE CURRENCY?

ESWAR S. PRASAD
VERA SONGWE

BROOKINGS INSTITUTION PRESS
Washington, D.C.

Copyright © 2021
THE BROOKINGS INSTITUTION
1775 Massachusetts Avenue, N.W.
Washington, D.C. 20036
www.brookings.edu

The Brookings Institution is a private nonprofit organization devoted to research, education, and publication on important issues of domestic and foreign policy. Its principal purpose is to bring the highest quality independent research and analysis to bear on current and emerging policy problems. Interpretations or conclusions in Brookings publications should be understood to be solely those of the authors.

Library of Congress Control Number: 2021938519

ISBN 9780815738534 (pbk)
ISBN 9780815738541 (ebook)

9 8 7 6 5 4 3 2 1

Typeset in Minion Pro

Composition by Elliott Beard

CONTENTS

ACKNOWLEDGMENTS

We are grateful to Central Bank of Nigeria Governor Godwin Emefiele, BCEAO Governor Tiémoko Meyliet Koné, Ghana's Minister of Finance Kenneth Ofori-Atta, various other finance ministers and central bank governors from the African region, as well as other officials and staff of BCEAO, the Central Bank of Nigeria, the Bank of Ghana, and the West African Monetary Institute for graciously sharing their perspectives and insights on the topics discussed in this book. We also thank Brahima Coulibaly, Bakary Dosso, Jeffrey Frankel, Philip Lane, and Momodou Saho for their helpful comments on various papers related to this project. Tsenguunjav Byambasuren, Sreyoshi Das, Tilahun Emiru, Michael Wenye Li, Yang Liu, Haven Yang, Eva Zhang, and Yujin Zhang provided excellent research assistance at various stages of this project. Finally, and most importantly, we owe a huge debt of gratitude to our families for their unstinting support and encouragement during the writing of this book.

REGIONAL INTEGRATION
IN
WEST AFRICA

1

Introduction and Overview

The leaders of the fifteen member countries of the Economic Community of West African States (ECOWAS) had set a goal of achieving a monetary and currency union by the end of 2020. With 2020 proving to be an exceptionally difficult year, the timing has been deferred, but the leaders' aspiration to form such a union remains in place. While member countries have made progress toward this goal, there are many challenges to attaining the requisite degree of macroeconomic convergence and establishing an adequate institutional framework. Whatever the eventual timing, this is an ambitious goal and has potentially significant implications for economic integration within the region. It also has important lessons for the African continent as a whole, particularly as the continent takes on a more aggressive trade integration strategy.

Monetary unions, as such, are not an end in themselves. They are a means to an end. This book provides an overview of the literature on monetary unions, with a special emphasis on emerging and developing market economies and the challenges involved in ensuring the durability and stability of such unions. The particular challenges facing ECOWAS, given the differences in current monetary and exchange rate regimes among countries in the region, will be examined. With accelerated economic integration, mon-

1

etary stability, and enhanced growth as the final objectives, this book studies how a monetary union could contribute to the attainment of these ends.[1]

Focusing on stability and growth as the overarching objectives, the book provides a detailed analytical evaluation of alternative exchange rate regimes and their relative benefits and complexities given the structure of the ECOWAS region. Although the book does not aim to flesh out the specific details of the monetary policy framework, the connection between exchange rate policy and monetary policy regimes is discussed in the context of currency unions. Some parallels are also drawn from other regions.

Finally, the book contains a discussion of the institutional framework as well as broader aspects of economic and political integration that will be required to underpin a stable and durable currency union.

ECONOMIC BACKGROUND

ECOWAS comprises a set of countries at different stages of development, as measured by per capita incomes. The fifteen countries span a wide range of per capita incomes, from US$400–US$700 per annum (Niger, Sierra Leone, and Togo) to about US$1,500 (Côte d'Ivoire, Senegal), with three significant outliers—Nigeria at US$2,222, Ghana at US$2,223, and Cabo Verde at US$3,599 (see table 1-1). Six of the fifteen could be regarded as middle-income countries (annual per capita income of at least US$1,000 per annum), while the others are low income. These differences remain quite large if one uses purchasing power parity (PPP) rather than market exchange rates to compare per capita incomes. In 2018, PPP per capita incomes ranged from US$1,081 in Niger to US$5,358 in Nigeria, US$5,735 in Ghana, and US$6,503 in Cabo Verde. Six countries have PPP-adjusted per capita incomes in the US$1,000–US$2,000 range.[2]

The proposed currency zone also has wide size disparities among its economies. Nigeria, which is now the largest economy in Africa, accounts for 66.7 percent of GDP in ECOWAS (at market exchange rates). Ghana and Côte d'Ivoire account for another 10 percent and 6.6 percent, respectively. The five smallest economies (Cabo Verde, the Gambia, Guinea Bissau, Liberia, Sierra Leone) together account for less than 2 percent of ECOWAS GDP. The disparities in terms of population are smaller—Ghana and Nigeria together account for 60 percent of the total population in the ECOWAS region. Along with Côte d'Ivoire, the three countries account for two-thirds of the ECOWAS population (for comparison, their combined share of ECOWAS

TABLE 1-1. Key Economic Data (2019)

Country	Per cap income (USD, current price)	Nominal GDP (USD billion)	Share of GDP (percent)	Population (millions)	Share of population (percent)	Growth and inflation in 2019		Growth and inflation 2009–2019 average	
						GDP growth (percent)	CPI inflation (percent)	GDP growth (percent)	CPI inflation (percent)
Benin*	1217	14.4	2.1	11.8	3.0	6.4	-0.9	4.5	1.2
Burkina Faso*	718	14.6	2.2	20.3	5.2	5.7	-3.2	5.7	0.6
Cabo Verde	3599	2.0	0.3	0.6	0.1	5.5	1.1	2.4	1.2
Côte d'Ivoire*	1691	44.4	6.6	26.3	6.8	6.9	0.8	6.0	1.4
The Gambia	755	1.8	0.3	2.3	0.6	6.0	7.1	3.0	6.0
Ghana	2223	67.1	10.0	30.2	7.8	6.1	7.2	6.5	11.4
Guinea	981	13.4	2.0	13.6	3.5	5.6	9.5	5.3	11.1
Guinea Bissau*	786	1.4	0.2	1.8	0.5	4.6	0.2	3.9	1.0
Liberia	704	3.2	0.5	4.6	1.2	-2.5	27.0	3.3	11.4
Mali*	924	17.6	2.6	19.1	4.9	5.1	-0.6	4.4	1.3
Niger*	405	9.4	1.4	23.3	6.0	5.8	-2.5	5.7	0.7
Nigeria	2222	446.5	66.7	201.0	51.9	2.2	11.4	4.2	11.8
Senegal*	1428	23.9	3.6	16.8	4.3	5.3	1.0	4.8	0.7
Sierra Leone	547	4.2	0.6	7.7	2.0	5.1	14.8	4.4	9.4
Togo*	671	5.5	0.8	8.2	2.1	5.3	0.7	5.7	1.5
Total		669.6	100.0	387.5	100.0				
Average	1258					4.9	4.9	4.7	4.7
Weighted Avg.	1986					3.4	8.7	4.6	9.6

Data Source: IMF World Economic Outlook (October 2019 and April 2020).

Notes: Weighted averages are weighted by 2019 nominal GDP in U.S. dollars. Asterisks indicate members of WAEMU.

GDP is 83 percent). Six countries (Cabo Verde, the Gambia, Guinea Bissau, Liberia, Sierra Leone, Togo) have populations below 10 million and, together, account for 7 percent of the total population in ECOWAS.

The ECOWAS region has experienced relatively robust growth over the last decade (see table 1-1). The cross-sectional mean of annual GDP growth over the period 2009–19 was 4.7 percent, with Ghana's annual growth rate of 6.5 percent topping the group. In 2019, most countries had growth in the 5–6 percent range, although Nigeria registered only 2.2 percent growth, and Liberia's economy experienced a contraction. The COVID-19 pandemic has adversely affected growth in 2020 in all of these countries.

Figure 1-1 shows that Nigeria has been a major contributor to growth in ECOWAS over the last decade. The two panels of this figure show that, whether measured at market exchange rates or purchasing power parity (PPP) exchange rates, the relative importance of Nigeria to overall GDP growth is substantial. Figure 1-2 confirms that Nigeria accounted for two-thirds of overall ECOWAS GDP growth over the period 2009–19. Excluding the four recent years, 2016–19, when growth in Nigeria was negative or weak, this share rises to three-fourths. Ghana has accounted for about 14 percent of overall ECOWAS growth, while the contribution of the WAEMU countries was 13 percent over the period 2009–15, but rose to 20 percent if the subsequent four years are included.

These disparities in size and levels of economic development, as well as in the structures of their economies, pose some important challenges—both technical ones and in terms of governance—in creating a unified monetary zone for ECOWAS. Moreover, eight of the ECOWAS countries are already conjoined in a long-standing currency union—the West African Economic and Monetary Union (WAEMU), which, in turn, is part of the CFA franc zone.[3] The CFA franc is pegged to the euro. One other ECOWAS country (Cabo Verde) has a currency that is also pegged to the euro, while the remainder have a broad range of monetary and currency arrangements. This diversity adds a number of technical and operational challenges to creating a well-functioning and durable monetary union that can deliver economic benefits to the people of the ECOWAS community. At the same time, it should be recognized that the countries of the ECOWAS region represent one of the more integrated regional blocs on the continent. Another perspective on the issues discussed in this book is that they are about ways to build upon and intensify this integration.

FIGURE 1-1. Decomposition of Annual ECOWAS GDP Growth
(in percent)

A. Market exchange rates

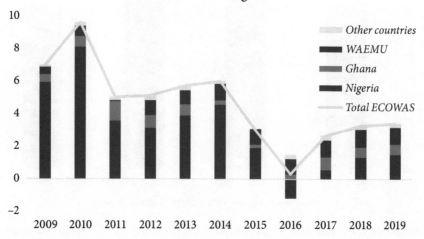

B. PPP exchange rates

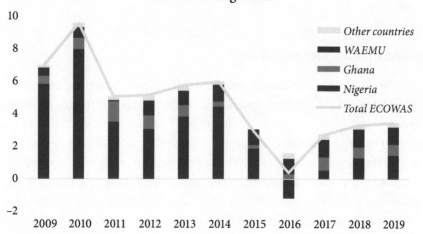

Notes: This figure shows aggregate real GDP growth in ECOWAS, along with the growth contributions of key countries and country groups. Panel A is based on real GDP growth in constant 2010 U.S. dollars at market exchange rates. Panel B is based on real GDP in constant 2011 U.S. dollars at PPP exchange rates.

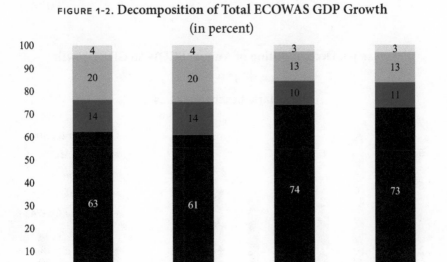

FIGURE 1-2. Decomposition of Total ECOWAS GDP Growth
(in percent)

■ Nigeria   ■ Ghana   ■ WAEMU   ▪ Other Countries

Notes: This figure breaks down aggregate real GDP growth in ECOWAS over the indicated periods into contributions of key countries and country groups. The first and third columns are based on real GDP growth in constant 2010 U.S. dollars at market exchange rates. The second and fourth columns are based on real GDP in constant 2011 U.S. dollars at PPP exchange rates.

ANALYTICAL FRAMEWORK

The literature on optimum currency areas (OCA) has identified some key criteria for a successful currency union, including the symmetry or similarity of shocks across countries, mobility of factors of production, openness to trade and finance, and degree of economic diversification. Each of these criteria will be analyzed in the upcoming chapters. Countries within a currency union can benefit from the "halo" effect stemming from one or more strong anchor countries that have disciplined macroeconomic and structural policies. This can reduce borrowing costs, macroeconomic volatility, and vulnerability to external shocks. For countries with high inflation and weak central banks that lack credibility, there are benefits to giving up autonomy over monetary policy, particularly if joining a currency union also increases fiscal policy discipline. Similarly, pooling foreign exchange reserves among currency union members can reduce individual countries' exposure to capital flow volatility.

Currency unions, if successful, have many potential benefits, which are described in chapter 2. Elimination of exchange rate risk within the currency union can have a positive effect on trade and investment flows within the region and, ultimately, growth. Indeed, as noted in chapter 3, the ongoing trade integration under the African Continental Free Trade Agreement initiative and policies to encourage factor mobility within ECOWAS could bode well for such a union.

There are also costs to forming a monetary union. With member countries having different production and economic structures, the loss of a key adjustment mechanism—independent currency and monetary policies— puts a significant burden on other policies. Fiscal transfers among countries, triggered by mechanisms to offset country-specific shocks, could spark political tensions if these are not mediated through a robust and trusted governance framework for the zone. Moreover, in the absence of adequate institutional safeguards and internal adjustment mechanisms (including labor and product market flexibility), the zone is only as strong as its weakest link.

Chapter 4 looks at the basic macroeconomic and structural prerequisites for a currency union. It will focus on the convergence criteria options, given the considerable differences in the structures of the ECOWAS economies. There is limited co-movement of GDP growth and inflation across ECOWAS countries. Terms-of-trade shocks are a key driver of economic fluctuations in most ECOWAS countries, accounting for a significant share of the variation in GDP growth and inflation. However, these shocks are not symmetric across the region, with a particularly strong asymmetry between the terms-of-trade shocks faced by Nigeria and WAEMU.

The conditions for an OCA are rarely fully met, even in existing currency unions, so ECOWAS is hardly an exception. Chapter 4 will look at other mechanisms that are essential for the currency union's ability to withstand aggregate shocks as well as shocks that affect countries asymmetrically. These mechanisms include (1) flexible product and labor markets, (2) labor mobility across countries and wage flexibility within countries, (3) mechanisms for sharing risk, and (4) a fiscal transfer system. All of these areas present major challenges for ECOWAS policymakers.

Initial conditions and congruence of macroeconomic conjunctures are also important for a successful currency union. ECOWAS leaders have determined a set of criteria—four main indicators and two ancillary ones—to assess macroeconomic convergence. Progress on meeting these criteria has been mixed. There are significant risks to moving forward with a currency union if the agreed-upon criteria are not met by all countries. This could reduce the credibility of the currency zone and would, at the outset, undermine the enforcement mechanisms intended to ensure consistency of economic policies across member countries. Moreover, as the world economy becomes more interconnected through trade and financial linkages, the potential vulnerability of ECOWAS member countries to external demand and financing shocks might need to be incorporated into a set of additional convergence criteria. The COVID-19 pandemic that ravaged the world economy in 2020, with particularly devastating effects on low-income countries, serves as an important cautionary note about shocks that could test the resiliency of a currency union.

Keeping all these caveats in mind, chapter 5 provides an analytical exploration of what alternative exchange rate regime and monetary policy framework might be suitable for an ECOWAS currency union. Based on the characteristics of ECOWAS economies, especially the high degree of exposure to terms of trade and other external shocks, a flexible exchange rate regime, along with a nominal anchor provided by an inflation targeting regime, would be a good option. This combination would help secure stability in the form of low inflation, with the flexible exchange rate providing a buffer against external shocks. Welfare calculations using a simple dynamic general equilibrium model bolster this conclusion.

This framework could be supplemented with a "leaning against the wind" option for exchange rate management. This option entails limiting short-term exchange rate volatility while not fundamentally resisting, through foreign exchange market intervention, market pressures pushing the currency in one direction or the other. Many emerging central banks, such as the Reserve Bank of India, explicitly or implicitly use this approach, recognizing that it can be counterproductive to resist sustained market pressures on a country's currency but that foreign exchange markets also tend to overshoot when market sentiments shift. The main objective of this approach is to use selective, symmetric, and temporary foreign exchange market intervention to mitigate such overshooting behavior and the policy complications resulting from it, while avoiding sustained, one-sided intervention.[4]

For all its benefits, such a regime is not without risks. A more flexible exchange rate and open capital account can make a developing economy more vulnerable to global financial cycles, including monetary policy spillovers from advanced economies that can trigger capital flow volatility. Exchange rate volatility can impose stresses on public finances and corporate balance sheets in the presence of significant levels of foreign currency debt. Fiscal dominance can also threaten price stability in the absence of a robust nominal anchor such as a fixed exchange rate.

There are a number of significant operational challenges to combining into a union a set of countries that have disparate levels of economic development, different monetary policy frameworks, and fragmented factor markets. The economic dominance of Nigeria—by far the largest country in the proposed currency zone in terms of both GDP and population—and its inevitable role as the anchor country pose additional challenges. For instance, Nigeria might face some policy constraints since the overall stability of the currency union could depend on the credibility and discipline of its policies.

There are substantial differences across ECOWAS countries in terms of their present exchange rate and monetary arrangements, which could create some transitional risks. Moreover, the disparities in capital account openness could complicate the management of whatever exchange rate regime is chosen for the eventual currency union.

Chapter 6 examines how a common ECOWAS currency regime and monetary policy framework might function. The experiments and analysis in this section show that, based on the degree of divergence in current practices, it will be essential but challenging to develop a consensus among ECOWAS members about the relative importance of variables such as inflation, output gaps, and exchange rate fluctuations in setting policy rates. Even with a consensus on these issues, there could be difficulties in formulating a common set of monetary and exchange rate policies for ECOWAS. First, any policy rule for ECOWAS that takes into account relative country sizes will be dominated by economic conditions in Nigeria. Second, the differences in economic structures and effects of external shocks imply that optimal policy rules look quite different for Nigeria than for WAEMU and Ghana. Third, and following from the second point, the desirable policy rate settings for Nigeria are likely to be quite different from those for WAEMU and Ghana, which could make it complicated to use a common exchange rate regime and monetary policy framework.

BUILDING AND HARMONIZING
RESILIENT POLICY FRAMEWORKS AND INSTITUTIONS

Chapter 7 makes the case that a strong institutional framework is needed to underpin the currency zone, in addition to harmonizing specific elements of institutions within each country. The main elements include:

- Uniformity of trade regimes; elimination of trade barriers

- Effective mechanism for gathering macroeconomic and other data

- A robust multilateral surveillance mechanism with "teeth" to deal with deviations from jointly agreed-upon criteria

- Harmonized and well-coordinated banking supervision and regulation

- Harmonization of capital and current account regulations

- Risk-pooling mechanism to deal with asymmetric external shocks

- Regional payment system

The recent experience of the eurozone suggests that a currency zone would be fortified by a broader economic union, including a banking union, a unified pan-zone financial regulatory system, and harmonized institutions underpinning the functioning of labor and product markets. These are long-term considerations for ECOWAS leaders. It is also worth considering the alternative approach taken by Asian economies, which have attempted to foster greater regional trade and financial integration without forming a currency union. Ancillary issues relevant for making growth in the ECOWAS region robust and sustainable, and for spreading the benefits of growth more evenly, include (1) regional financial market development and integration, and (2) raising financial inclusion through traditional as well as new technologies.

Another key challenge is related to the harmonization of monetary policy frameworks. The transition path to a common central bank will require a number of institutional and operational features to be determined and agreed upon in advance, particularly in order to build credibility for the monetary policy operations of the new central bank. These considerations, in addition to the monetary policy framework itself, include:

- Definition of price stability

- Measurement of economic activity, including output gaps and labor market outcomes, for the entire zone

- Governance, legitimacy, and accountability of a cross-national central bank

- Effective communication with market participants

Chapter 8 concludes and provides an overall assessment of the ECOWAS single currency project. It highlights the ambitious but potentially beneficial nature of the project as well as the significant costs, operational challenges, and transitional risks associated with it. With an unwavering commitment to building resilient policy and robust institutions, the overall objective of building a prosperous ECOWAS region is possible, and the currency union could be a desirable element of a strategy to promote growth and prosperity.

While the project took a backseat in 2020–2021 as Africa and the world had to turn attention to coping with the economic ravages wrought by the COVID-19 pandemic, the relevance of the issues discussed in this book has in fact been intensified by recent developments. During the pandemic, advanced economies used their central banks to provide extensive liquidity support to their economies and stave off an even deeper global economic crisis. African countries called for a $100 billion stimulus to respond to the pandemic, but lacked the tools to finance such an injection of capital into their economies. Would strong regional central banks or even a continental central bank have helped? The regional experience of the ECOWAS provides some indication of what would be needed to accomplish monetary integration. But it also highlights the difficulties the continent faces and some fundamental issues that must be resolved to promote resilience in the region and to foster alternative avenues to regional integration.

2

Basic Analytical Considerations

This chapter begins with a review of the relative benefits of fixed versus floating exchange rate regimes. It then reviews the potential benefits and challenges of a currency union, first in general and then with specific reference to developing economies. This will set the basis for a discussion in chapter 3 about the possible gains from trade integration that could be realized from an ECOWAS currency union. This chapter then provides a brief exploration of analytical criteria for an optimum currency area (OCA). Chapter 4 will explore how the proposed currency union fares in terms of these criteria.

FIXED VERSUS FLOATING EXCHANGE RATES

Fixed exchange rates provide a stable nominal anchor for monetary policy. Many developing economies that had fallen into high-inflation traps succeeded in escaping them when their stabilization programs included a visible commitment to a target for the exchange rate. The academic argument for such a nominal anchor for monetary policy is that there can be an inflationary bias when monetary policy is set by governments with full discretion.[1] A central bank that wants to fight inflation can make its commitment more credible by fixing the exchange rate or, in extreme circumstances, even giving up its currency altogether (dollarization). Workers, firm managers, and others who set wages and prices then perceive that inflation will be low in the future, because the currency peg will constrain expansionary monetary policy. When workers and firm managers have low expectations of inflation, they set their wages and prices accordingly. The result is that the country is able to attain a lower level of inflation for any given level of output.

This argument assumes that the currency to which the domestic country is considering pegging is itself stable. For countries in Latin America and the Caribbean, the currency in question is usually the U.S. dollar; for those in Europe and Africa, it is more likely to be the euro (since 1999; before 1999, it was the deutsche mark or French franc).

Another argument in favor of fixed exchange rates is the positive effect on international trade. Exchange rate variability creates uncertainty, discouraging exports and imports; hedging against this uncertainty can be costly. Furthermore, dealing in multiple currencies incurs transaction costs. Fixing a country's exchange rate relative to a major trading partner country can encourage international trade, at least with that country. If that trading partner country happens to be a big one with a more stable exchange rate of its own, there can also be a significant positive effect on the home country's trade with the rest of the world.

Similarly, exchange rate risk and currency transaction costs act as barriers to cross-border asset trade and banking flows. Eliminating them by fixing the exchange rate can promote financial integration.

Skepticism about the trade-enhancing effects of fixed exchange rates has been based on three arguments.[2] First, in theory, nominal exchange rate volatility merely reflects variability in economic fundamentals: if it is suppressed in the foreign exchange market, it will show up somewhere else, in particular in the variability of goods prices. Second, currency risk can be hedged using forward markets or other derivative markets. Third, is it difficult to empirically discern an adverse effect of increased exchange rate volatility on trade.

These arguments are not clear cut. First, nominal exchange rate changes are often unrelated to changes in macroeconomic fundamentals and appear to be the cause rather than the result of real exchange rate variability.[3] Second, there are no derivative markets for the currencies of many smaller economies, such as most of those in Africa. Even where such markets exist, liquidity is limited and hedging costs tend to be high. Third, there is now a body of evidence documenting the negative effects of exchange rate variability on trade volumes.

Some relevant econometric evidence is drawn from empirical analysis of gravity models, which suggest that reducing exchange rate variability has a statistically significant—albeit quantitatively modest—positive effect on trade. Institutional fixes such as currency boards or dollarization have a bigger effect, and currency unions have the biggest effect of all. For instance, Rose (2000) finds that two members of a common currency area tend to trade as much as three times more with each other, compared to an otherwise similarly situated pair of countries. Using a time series sample, which includes a number of countries that left currency unions, Glick and Rose (2002) find trade among the members twice as high in the currency union period as afterward. Frankel and Rose (2002) find that for each 1 percent in trade openness (measured by the ratio of trade to GDP) resulting from a common currency, GDP goes up by one-third of a percent.[4]

FLEXIBLE EXCHANGE RATES

Flexible exchange rates have a number of advantages of their own. One key advantage is that it allows a country to retain an independent monetary policy, even if that country has few capital controls and is integrated into international financial markets. A second advantage is that the nominal exchange rate acts as a useful shock absorber in response to certain types of shocks, especially shocks to export demand. Third, especially compared to extreme fixed exchange rate regimes such as currency boards and dollarization, a central bank that operates under a flexible exchange rate maintains its seigniorage revenues and lender of last resort privileges.

Some of these advantages of a flexible exchange rate regime have been the subject of recent debate in the context of developing and emerging market economies. Hélène Rey (2015) has questioned whether exchange rate flexibility, in fact, insulates countries from foreign shock and whether it allows them to choose their own interest rates even when, for example, the Federal Reserve raises U.S. interest rates. By contrast, Klein and Shambaugh (2016) find empirical support for the traditional view that "a moderate amount of exchange rate flexibility does allow for some degree of monetary autonomy, especially in emerging and developing economies." Di Giovanni and Shambaugh (2008) find that, while foreign interest rates have a negative impact on domestic GDP in pegged countries, flexible exchange rates insulate against them. Aizenman, Chinn, and Ito (2010, 2011) find that exchange rate stability is associated with less monetary independence and more output volatility.

Obstfeld (2015) finds that the correlation between local and U.S. short-term interest rates falls to zero for countries with flexible exchange rates.[5]

For African countries, fluctuations in the terms of trade (the ratio of export prices to import prices) are an especially important source of external shocks. The biggest sources of exogenous terms-of-trade shocks tend to be changes in the world prices of oil, minerals, or agricultural commodities that affect countries specializing in the exports of those products. This factor is relevant for almost all African countries. Other things being equal, countries with more volatile terms of trade benefit from exchange rate regimes that can at least partially help absorb those shocks. A number of studies have confirmed empirically that in the presence of large terms-of-trade shocks, economic performance tends to be better in countries with floating exchange rates than in countries with fixed exchange rates. Céspedes and Velasco (2012), for example, examine 107 major country commodity boom-bust cycles, and find that the output loss from a given commodity price decline is smaller the more flexible is the exchange rate.[6]

POLICYMAKERS' DILEMMA

Given all of this conflicting evidence on the pros and cons of fixed versus flexible exchange rates, what is the right solution? To address this question from a different perspective, some studies have classified countries according to their de facto exchange rate regime and then tested which categories have superior economic performance, judged usually by growth and/or inflation.[7] This literature is largely inconclusive. Some studies find that floating works best, some that institutionally fixed rates work best, and some that an intermediate regime works best.

Why do papers in this literature yield such different answers? One reason is that the classification schemes do not correspond to each other.[8] To that extent, it is no surprise that various authors get different answers as to the performance of different categories of exchange rate regimes. A more important reason, which is crucial for the analysis in this book, is that the answer is highly dependent on a country's specific circumstances. No single exchange rate regime is right for all countries. We need a framework for thinking about the characteristics that suit a country or other geographic area for choosing fixed, floating, or intermediate exchange rate regimes. This requires a better understanding of the characteristics that determine the relative weights that should be placed on the advantages and disadvantages of different regimes considered above.

FIXED EXCHANGE RATES AND CURRENCY UNIONS

The binary choice between fixed and flexible is convenient for textbook purposes, but oversimplifies the range of options considerably. The full range runs from free floating—not relevant for most developing countries—to an institutionally fixed regime such as adopting a foreign currency as legal tender domestically. A wide variety of intermediate regimes, such as target zones and adjustable pegs, are arrayed along the spectrum in between the polar extremes of free floating and currency unions.

For many African countries, and for the purposes of this project, the relevant choice is between joining a monetary union and retaining a degree of flexibility. What difference does it make if the commitment is to a monetary union rather than a simple declaration of a fixed exchange rate? For one thing, many formally declared pegs are best classified in practice as adjustable pegs, because they last only until they are put under strain, often due to a big shock.[9] Thus, one important way that a currency union differs from a fixed exchange rate is the relative permanence of the arrangement. A fixed exchange rate can always be changed. Of course, even the CFA franc devalued against the French franc in 1994.[10]

A monetary union has at least two advantages that are different from fixed exchange rates not just quantitatively but qualitatively. First, it avoids not only the speculative bubbles that may sometimes afflict floating exchange rates, but also the speculative attacks that sometimes afflict pegged exchange rates. Second, a country that joins a currency union usually gains the right to some sort of representation in the decisionmaking of the union's central bank.

The decision to join a monetary union is not permanent and irrevocable, but the cases of countries leaving such a union, or the union dissolving entirely, are rare. For an individual country, this is a way of making a more credible commitment to monetary discipline than through a unilateral fixed exchange rate. The near-permanence of a currency union is, however, a double-edged sword for monetary policy. It does make inflation-fighting more credible, but also virtually eliminates the possibility of responding to even a very severe negative shock. Greece probably regretted the decision to join the euro when it could not devalue or lower interest rates even in response to a crisis as severe as the one it suffered in 2010.[11]

Countries that form a monetary union also run into some problems that do not arise from ordinary fixed exchange rates. If responsibility for fiscal policy remains at the national level, moral hazard can arise as individual governments run up excessive levels of debt, because they and their creditors feel that they will likely be bailed out by other members of the union in the event of a fiscal crisis. The architects of EMU recognized and addressed this danger by setting limits on members' budget deficits and debt levels. But many members violated the limits, precipitating the eurozone debt crisis that erupted in 2010. One can imagine similar problems of fiscal moral hazard afflicting an African currency union.[12]

POTENTIAL BENEFITS OF A CURRENCY UNION

There are many benefits to a currency union among ECOWAS members. It can enhance trade and investment flows in the region, bring discipline to the macroeconomic and structural policies of member countries, and provide a degree of stability against external shocks.

Elimination of exchange rate risk, along with harmonization of trade regimes and other relevant aspects of a monetary union, could provide a significant boost to trade flows within the region. Such trade would involve not just final products but also intermediate inputs if businesses start building supply chains within the zone. An extensive academic literature has documented the positive relationship between lower levels of exchange rate volatility and higher levels of trade and investment flows. These effects are stronger in the context of a currency union, since businesses and investors can benefit from the elimination of currency risk within the union, so long as the member countries' commitment to the policies necessary to sustain the union is seen as credible.[13] This could lead to greater investment flows in the region. Thus, a currency union can also promote broader economic integration among its constituent countries.

Countries within a currency union can benefit from the "halo" effect of one or more strong anchor countries that have disciplined macroeconomic and structural policies. This, in addition to the group-monitoring effect (countries in the group exercise influence to keep any single country from pursuing undisciplined policies), can reduce borrowing costs, macroeconomic volatility, and vulnerability to external shocks.

For instance, countries with high inflation that have central banks with low levels of credibility in controlling inflation can benefit from giving up autonomy over monetary policy, particularly if joining a currency union also requires more disciplined fiscal policy. Similarly, pooling of foreign exchange reserves among the members of the currency union can reduce the exposure each of them faces to capital flow volatility that is attributable to shifts in investor sentiment (rather than weak macroeconomic fundamentals). Of course, this is relevant only if the countries face idiosyncratic (country-specific) shocks rather than common shocks, such as a sudden stop or reversal of capital flows to the entire zone.

ALTERNATIVES TO A CURRENCY UNION: THE CHIANG MAI INITIATIVE

Moreover, there are ways of achieving some of these objectives without joining a currency union. Asia provides a case in point. The Chiang Mai Initiative launched in 2000 was set up by a group of Asian economies to promote regional insurance. The subsequent Chiang Mai Initiative Multilateralization (CMIM) involved a more explicit reserve pooling arrangement. The CMIM provides a relatively limited amount of unfettered access (30 percent of the withdrawal limit negotiated by each country under the arrangement), with higher levels of access to funds from the regional pool subject to the country agreeing to a program with the IMF. The CMIM has a regional macroeconomic surveillance unit—the ASEAN+3 Macroeconomic Research Office (AMRO). However, there are no explicit benchmarks for macroeconomic performance that individual countries are required to adhere to. Despite the existence of a regional safety net, most countries in the region have, for the most part, relied on self-insurance through the accumulation of foreign exchange reserves. This might be because of the relatively modest size of the reserve pool and the conditions attached to its use.

COSTS, CHALLENGES, RISKS

There are also important costs to forming a monetary union. With member countries having rather different production and economic structures, the loss of an adjustment mechanism—in the form of an independent currency and monetary policy—puts a significant burden on other policies.

The experience of the eurozone also points to an important lesson: in the absence of adequate institutional safeguards and internal adjustment mechanisms (including labor and product market flexibility), the zone is only as strong as its weakest link.

In weighing the potential costs and benefits of a currency union, it is worth reviewing the basic characteristics that Robert Mundell had identified for an OCA. Those criteria (discussed in more detail later in this chapter) include the free mobility of the factors of production within the area. An additional criterion is the symmetry of macroeconomic shocks, both domestic and external, that the countries in the area are subject to. A lower degree of symmetry, coupled with the absence of the exchange rate buffer that can mitigate the consequences of country-specific shocks, imposes a greater burden on other adjustment mechanisms.

A higher degree of factor mobility can, to some extent, compensate for the effects of asymmetric shocks hitting countries within an OCA. However, it is prudent to think of alternative adjustment mechanisms to absorb such shocks. Consider the United States, which, in effect, is a currency union comprised of its states. The United States has a common monetary policy and a high degree of factor mobility since capital and labor markets are well integrated across states. Even in the case of the United States, the tax and transfer system plays an important role in cushioning individual states from shocks that they are exposed to. For instance, a fall in oil prices has a negative effect on oil-producing states and positive effects on others. A rise in unemployment in the negatively affected states can be offset by an increase in federal transfers to those states and a reduction in their federal tax payments.

Such fiscal transfers within a currency union can create political tensions, particularly if such transfers are persistent. This situation can be exacerbated if there is a perception that countries that are net recipients of such transfers are unwilling to undertake the difficult reforms necessary to bring their macroeconomic and structural policies in line with those of other countries in the union.

The wide dispersion of living standards and employment opportunities (which is related to both relative economic size and relative growth rates) could create potential political tensions within the currency union if there were to be free movement of labor. Moreover, such free movement may not be considered feasible or even desirable, especially in the short term. This imposes a greater burden on other adjustment mechanisms in response to asymmetric shocks hitting countries within the proposed union.

A DEVELOPING COUNTRY PERSPECTIVE ON THE
BENEFITS AND COSTS OF A CURRENCY UNION

The benefits and costs discussed above may need some modifications in the context of developing countries. To begin with, it is worth reviewing developing country currency unions to see if they hold any lessons for ECOWAS. However, other than the CFA franc zone, the number of currency unions among developing countries is limited. The Eastern Caribbean Currency Union, set up in 1981, comprises Anguilla, Antigua and Barbuda, Dominica, Grenada, Montserrat, Saint Kitts and Nevis, Saint Lucia, Saint Vincent, and the Grenadines. The Common Monetary Area, set up in 1986, includes South Africa, Namibia, Lesotho, and Swaziland. These currency unions have, at a minimum, been durable, although the analytical evidence on their welfare benefits is limited.

In the aftermath of the Asian financial crisis, a few East Asian economies considered forming a currency union, partly as a mechanism to fend off external shocks, especially those associated with the volatility of capital flows to the region. The Japanese government lent some support to the concept of an Asian Monetary Unit (AMU), a currency basket computed as a weighted average of the currencies of the ten ASEAN economies plus China, Korea, and Japan.[14] The AMU, in conjunction with a proposed new organization called the Asian Monetary Fund (AMF) that was envisioned as the regional equivalent of the IMF, was intended to underpin the currency union.

However, neither the AMU nor the AMF came into being, partly on account of political considerations related to governance and partly due to concerns about the balance of power among different countries within the union. Instead, as noted earlier, regional risk-sharing mechanisms such as the Chiang Mai Initiative took on some of the proposed functions of the currency union. Similarly, as a catalyst for regional financial market development, the Asian Bond Fund Initiative became a substitute for more direct financial integration through a currency union.[15]

Appendix A lists the extensive trade and financial arrangements among Asian countries. There is a great deal of academic evidence, both empirical and based on simulation exercises, that these regional trade agreements helped boost trade flows within Asia.[16] Whether such regional trade and financial agreements have positive effects of the same magnitude as a currency union on trade flows and broader economic integration remains an open question. But it is clearly one that deserves careful consideration, especially in view of the establishment of the African Continental Free Trade Area. In particular, an initiative along the lines of the Asian Bond Fund could help spur financial market development in the region, in addition to providing a channel for regional savings to finance productive investment opportunities within the region.

Latin American countries have, on occasion, contemplated regional currency unions, but the disparate economic fortunes of countries in the region, along with concerns about both the quality of domestic governance and potential conflicts about the governance structure of any possible union, have stymied such efforts. Instead, some countries in the region, dealing with the scourge of high inflation or hyperinflation and central banks that lacked credibility, have often turned to more drastic solutions such as dollarization.

What, then, are the particular benefits that would lead developing countries, such as the members of ECOWAS, to contemplate a currency union? Many developing countries tend to have less credible central banks and weak public finances, both of which make it difficult to achieve and maintain low and stable inflation. Thus, a currency union with a strong central bank can serve as an anchor for inflation expectations within the zone.

Small, open developing economies tend to be vulnerable to capital flow volatility, which can put substantial stresses on their balance of payments. A currency union anchored by a foreign exchange reserve pooling arrangement among member countries could provide an additional buffer for individual countries in coping with sudden stops or reversals of capital inflows. On the other hand, such a pool of reserves will not provide protection against regional shocks that affect multiple countries in a currency union simultaneously, as is often the case.

A currency union can also serve as an external catalyst for labor and product market reforms in the member countries, since they would need adjustment mechanisms other than the exchange rate to respond to both domestic and external shocks. Such reforms can have significant positive welfare effects. In addition, a currency union can serve as an external disciplining device on fiscal policies.[17]

On the other hand, developing countries tend to have less diversified economies and are more prone to external shocks. Such shocks include fluctuations in the terms of trade (driven, for instance, by commodity price shocks) and capital flow surges and reversals. This can affect the cost-benefit calculus of joining a currency union, since the exchange rate serves as an important buffer against external shocks, especially in countries that have labor and product market rigidities. In the absence of robust governance mechanisms, a currency zone can also lead to more profligate fiscal behavior by certain countries on account of the presumption that there is a collective responsibility of all members in the zone for government debt issued by any of its member countries.

Thus, for developing countries, there are particular challenges to ensuring that the costs of a currency union do not outweigh the potential benefits. These challenges are likely to be more acute during the initial phases of the establishment of the currency zone (when member countries are working to align their macro and structural policies) and during times of global financial market stresses.

CURRENCY UNION CRITERIA: AN ANALYTICAL EXPLORATION

Building upon the work of Mundell, a number of optimal currency area criteria have been identified in the academic literature. The traditional literature on optimum currency areas (OCA) has focused on such criteria as the symmetry or similarity of shocks across countries, mobility of factors of production, openness to trade and finance, and degree of economic diversification.[18] OCAs are, in principle, characterized by the similarity of countries in terms of (1) their exposure to different types and sources of exogenous shocks, (2) amplitude and persistence of their business cycles, (3) their tolerance for inflation and commitment to fiscal discipline, and (4) the structure and degree of diversification of their economies. A high degree of factor mobility is also regarded as a desirable characteristic.

These criteria are seldom fully met in practice. Even a country such as the United States, which is, in effect, a set of state economies tied together into a currency union, does not fully meet all the criteria of an OCA. Hence, it is important to evaluate various adjustment mechanisms that are relevant for a currency union's ability to withstand aggregate shocks affecting the entire currency union, as well as shocks that affect the countries within the union asymmetrically.

The typical adjustment mechanisms are as follows:

   a. *Price and wage flexibility.* Flexibility of prices and wages within and across countries can help adjust to nation-specific as well as common shocks.

b. *Mobility of labor and capital.* A high level of factor market integration can offset the need for relative price adjustment (through nominal exchange rate changes) in response to country-specific shocks.

c. *Risk sharing.* Integrated financial markets can help smooth consumption flows in response to output disturbances. This can happen simply through portfolio diversification by economic agents within the zone if they have relatively cheap and unfettered access to investment opportunities across the zone.

d. *Fiscal system.* The tax and transfer system can reallocate resources across the zone in response to shocks that have asymmetric effects across members of the zone.

The recent experience of the eurozone suggests that a currency zone would be fortified by a broader economic union, including a banking union, a unified pan-zone financial regulatory system, and harmonized institutions underpinning the functioning of labor and product markets.

ENDOGENEITY OF OCA CRITERIA

Such characteristics as openness to trade and cyclical correlations can evolve over time, including in response to the formation of a currency union itself. Frankel and Rose (1998) point out the endogeneity of OCA criteria. They note, in particular, the endogeneity of two parameters, the intensity of intra-regional trade and the intra-regional correlation of shocks, with respect to the decision to enter a currency area. More specifically, they find that when a currency union promotes trade among its members, as documented in Rose (2000), there usually follows an increase in the correlation of shocks across members. Thus, a group of countries might satisfy these two criteria many years after forming a currency union, even if they did not satisfy them before forming the union. Calderón and Chong (2007) also find a significant effect of trade integration on business cycle correlations among developing countries, although the effect is not as strong as among advanced countries. The research that allows for the endogeneity of the OCA criteria has been labeled the "new" theory of optimum currency areas.[19]

Some authors have hypothesized that other parameters, particularly labor mobility and flexibility of labor and goods markets, might also be endogenous with respect to the decision to form a currency area. Labor mobility did go up among the eurozone members, for example. But hopes that the loss of the monetary policy tool would force all member countries in that currency union to reform their labor and goods markets proved unrealistic, at least until the extreme circumstances of the aftermath of the 2010 crisis in the euro periphery.

More work is needed to analyze the benefits of OCA for developing countries. In particular, the experience of Asia over the last three decades, which featured strong growth supported by rapid trade integration even without a currency union, deserves more attention. The next chapter examines what lessons this experience could have for ECOWAS. Europe's experience with a currency area indicates the importance of a robust governance system with a strong center. The Franco-German alliance is key to the eurozone's stability, although the two countries have sometimes differed in their philosophies about how the eurozone should be governed. The leaders of such an alliance in the ECOWAS could, for instance, include Nigeria, Ghana, and Côte d'Ivoire. These three countries have significantly different institutional structures, which could complicate effective governance.

3

Integration through Trade

Africa's share of global trade (2 percent) has been unimpressive over the past two decades, relative to the continent's share of the global population as well as of natural and other resources. Deepening trade integration, both within the continent and with the rest of the world, has therefore been a major preoccupation of countries in the region. The desire has led to the proliferation of Regional Trade Agreements (RTA) and subregional agreements in order to defragment the continent and integrate subregions into the global economy. While these agreements have led to improvements in intra-regional trade among some subregion countries in Africa, however, the extent of intra-regional trade perforation is still low relative to other regions. The African Continental Free Trade Area agreement now seeks to build one common regional trading block in order to benefit from scale and harmonization of processes to further accelerate intra-regional trade. The main vehicle, it is anticipated, will be through building regional supply chains and moving more value–adding production processes unto the continent.

This chapter discusses levels and trends in trade integration among the ECOWAS countries. The quest to deepen trade integration resulted in the ECOWAS Trade Liberalization Scheme (ETLS), aimed at boosting duty-free trade among countries in the subregion. The ETLS provides unrestricted market access that should foster economic integration within the regional bloc. However, progress on intra-regional trade integration has been unimpressive, given the low shares of intra-regional exports in total exports of ECOWAS member states.

There is scope for substantially greater trade integration within this group of countries. However, as the experience within the WAEMU group of countries indicates, trade integration will require more than just the formation of a currency union. This chapter will conclude with a review of a major recent continent-wide initiative, the African Continental Free Trade Area (AfCFTA) agreement, which could provide a good basis for promoting trade. The AfCFTA can help achieve a more equitable distribution of socioeconomic costs and benefits across all fifty-four countries in Africa, but this goal comes with the prerequisite of fostering domestic entrepreneurship, domestic resource mobilization, improving trade infrastructure and logistics, advancing political stability and peace, and establishing appropriate institutional structures and mechanisms.

STYLIZED FACTS ON INTRA-REGIONAL TRADE PERFORMANCE: A BRIEF OVERVIEW

Deepening economic cooperation at the regional level will require more than a single currency, as evidenced by the WAEMU experience, where intra–currency union trade flows are significantly below trade with the rest of the world (ROW) (see figure 3-1). The creation of monetary unions must be complemented by mutually beneficial trade agreements, investments in institutions to regulate and facilitate trade, as well as improvement in skills. The approach of the eurozone provides some useful lessons. Europe worked to consolidate its single market and achieve a high degree of trade integration before the establishment of the euro. The eurozone countries gradually built up an architecture of processes, institutions, and regulations. Even if the European project holds cautionary lessons for Africa as it failed to form a strong fiscal and political union, trade integration was achieved on the back of a strong institutional environment, macroeconomic stability, and commitment to free trade within the union.

A successful outcome of the formation of the WAEMU union is that membership has brought a great deal of monetary stability to countries in the union. WAEMU members contribute to the common pool of foreign exchange reserves, and the regional central bank, Banque Centrale des Etats

FIGURE 3-1. **Intra- and Extra-Zone Trade: WAEMU and Eurozone**

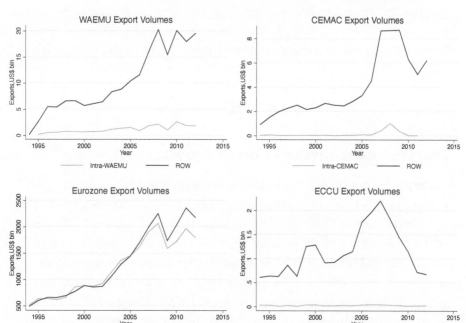

de l'Afrique de l'Ouest (BCEAO), sets the monetary policy of the union. The credibility of the currency peg to the euro has been strong, and the bank has done a good job of keeping consumer price inflation stable.

Despite the relatively favorable economic conditions in the WAEMU union, member countries need to address the factors constraining intra-regional trade, which remains at low levels. In addition to developing the financial sector as well as improving institutions and governance, WAEMU countries have to address inadequate transportation and energy infrastructure, which remain obstacles to reaping the full benefits of the common market.[1]

As this chapter shows, trade performance in the WAEMU and ECOWAS has remained broadly unchanged over the last decades, at a time when other countries were better able to take advantage of the global trend toward stronger trade interlinkages. This poses the question about how to improve and support better trade performance beyond creating a common currency. Research conducted at the United Nations Economic Commission for Africa (UNECA) suggest that the WAEMU and Central African Economic and Monetary Community (CEMAC) blocs have achieved better trade integration than would be expected on the basis of factors such as economic size, geographical proximity, common language, and the nominal exchange rate regime. Of course, it is difficult to separate the effects of a currency union from those of trade agreements among members of the union, so these results should be interpreted with caution. But the analysis also shows that intra-regional trade levels in these two blocs are below the levels achieved by other currency unions outside of Africa.

LIMITED TRADE INTEGRATION IN ECOWAS

The extent of trade flows is crucial in examining the pattern of trade and integration. Table 3-1 presents statistics on ECOWAS trade patterns as a percentage of total trade in 2010 and 2019. The majority of trade flows of ECOWAS countries is accounted for by trade with the European Union. This holds whether the trade flows are taken as values of exports or imports or total trade. It is interesting to note that between 2010 and 2019, ECOWAS trade with the United States declined significantly. The share of ECOWAS exports accounted for by the United States declined from 26 percent to just 5 percent over this period.[2] On the other hand, ECOWAS trade flows with India and China have increased as shares of the region's total trade. In 2019, India accounted for 22 percent of ECOWAS exports while China accounted for 9 percent.

At the intra-regional level, trade flows among ECOWAS member states have been disappointing, although the value of total trade accounted for by intra-ECOWAS trade increased marginally from about 9 percent in 2010 to 10 percent in 2019. It is also interesting to note that the share of intra-ECOWAS trade fell by 1 percentage point over this period while the corresponding share of exports rose by 4 percentage points.[3] Indeed, while the rising share of exports within the economic bloc suggests rising trade integration, the level of integration still remains modest, as ECOWAS countries still rely, to a large extent, on exports to countries outside the zone, given relative shares across the countries and regional blocs.

One question is whether these trade patterns are driven by Nigeria, which is, by far, the largest economy in ECOWAS. Table 3-2 shows results for ECOWAS trade patterns after excluding Nigeria. It can be seen that trade with Europe still accounts for the largest share. The level of intra-ECOWAS trade appears higher when Nigeria is excluded, but is still at a relatively low level. The share of exports to countries within the bloc shows a smaller increase than in table 3-1.

TABLE 3-1. ECOWAS Trade Patterns (as shares of total trade, in percent)

	Value of total trade		Value of exports		Value of imports	
	2010	2019	2010	2019	2010	2019
European Union	20.5	22.2	17.9	21.6	24.3	22.9
Of which: Euro Area	19.8	21.3	17.7	21.0	23.0	21.6
India	11.7	14.9	17.6	22.2	3.0	6.4
China	6.0	13.9	2.1	9.2	12.0	19.5
ECOWAS	8.7	10.1	8.3	11.6	9.3	8.3
United States	19.7	6.0	25.5	4.9	10.9	7.3

Data Source: Authors' calculations, based on IMF Direction of Trade Statistics data.

TABLE 3-2. ECOWAS Trade Patterns, Excluding Nigeria
(as shares of total trade, in percent)

	Value of total trade		Value of exports		Value of imports	
	2010	2019	2010	2019	2010	2019
European Union	26.6	20.9	24.2	15.3	28.4	25.9
Of which: Euro Area	25.4	19.5	23.3	14.6	26.9	24.0
ECOWAS, Excluding Nigeria	11.9	12.3	14.5	16.2	10.1	8.7
China	7.8	14.1	1.5	12.2	12.5	15.9
India	2.8	10.1	3.1	13.5	2.6	7.1
United States	6.1	4.4	5.7	3.6	6.3	5.1

Data Source: Authors' calculations, based on IMF Direction of Trade Statistics data.

CAN WAEMU BE USED AS A BENCHMARK FOR ASSESSING IMPLICATIONS OF CURRENCY UNION FOR TRADE INTEGRATION? A PRELIMINARY ANALYSIS

Zooming into a key subset of the ECOWAS countries, has the WAEMU currency union achieved better trade integration?

Similarly, while the share of exports within WAEMU economies increased to about 21 percent, it is still low. The 21 percent exports share in the union represents the highest share among WAEMU trading partners in 2019; the eight WAEMU member states exported more among themselves.

However, when combined with their share of imports in total trade, there is a drop. Members of the WAEMU import less from each other than they do from the European Union.

Table 3-3 presents WAEMU trade patterns in 2010 and 2019. Intra-CFA zone total trade accounted for only 14.6 percent of their overall trade in 2019 (see table 3-3). This is significantly lower than the over 60 percent share of intra-zone trade among eurozone economies with a common currency. Moreover, despite the absence of exchange rate volatility relative to the eurozone, the share of the WAEMU countries' total trade accounted for by the European Union fell by 2.8 percentage points from 2010 to 2019.[4] It is encouraging that the share of WAEMU exports accounted for by other WAEMU countries nearly doubled from 12 percent in 2010 to 21 percent in 2019. The share of intra-bloc trade of WAEMU imports has remained relatively stable at around 10 or 11 percent.

Since eight of the ECOWAS countries are already in a currency union, the benefit from an expansion of the currency union might be smaller than for a group of countries creating a new union. Expanding from WAEMU to an ECOWAS currency union would amount to a five-fold increase in GDP. Nevertheless, a monetary union by itself will deliver, at best, limited benefits unless it is accompanied by policies to reduce or eliminate trade barriers, particularly non-tariff bottlenecks within the zone.

TABLE 3-3. WAEMU Trade Patterns (as shares
of total trade, in percent)

	Value of total trade		Value of exports		Value of imports	
	2010	2019	2010	2019	2010	2019
European Union	27.4	24.6	26.4	18.7	28.2	29.3
WAEMU	11.3	14.6	11.9	20.7	10.9	9.7
United States	5.3	4.0	6.7	4.6	4.3	3.5
South Africa	4.5	2.1	7.2	2.8	2.5	1.5
India	2.7	5.9	3.7	7.0	1.9	5.0
Nigeria	8.6	4.9	5.2	3.7	11.1	5.9
Vietnam	0.8	1.9	0.7	3.3	0.9	0.8
Malaysia	1.0	1.3	1.1	1.7	0.9	0.9
China	7.8	8.9	1.7	3.0	12.3	13.8

Data Source: Authors' calculations, based on IMF Direction of Trade Statistics data.

Senegal provides a useful case study. The establishment of WAEMU has helped anchor low and stable inflation in Senegal, substantially reduced nominal exchange rate volatility (on a trade-weighted basis), and improved overall economic growth. A majority of Senegal's imports, roughly 43 percent in 2019, were from the European Union (see table 3-4), while the rest of WAEMU accounted for barely 2 percent. The share of Senegal's exports to WAEMU countries decreased from about 34 percent in 2010 to 30 percent in 2019. The lower trade integration with other WAEMU economies is reflected in the modest share of Senegal's overall trade accounted for by other WAEMU countries; this share declined from 2010 to 2019. The low share of Senegal's trade accounted for by other WAEMU countries suggests that one of the key benefits of being in a currency bloc—expansion of trade volumes within the bloc—have not been realized.

Notwithstanding the lackluster performance of ECOWAS and WAEMU, Africa's RTAs have in general experienced improvements in intra-zone trade. For instance, intra-regional trade shares in the Common Market for Eastern and Southern Africa (COMESA) and the Southern African Development Community (SADC) have increased by about 10 percentage points over the past decade. By contrast, about 95 percent of the trade of CEMAC countries is with the rest of the world; only 5 percent of their exports stays within Africa.

TABLE 3-4. **Senegal Trade Patterns (as shares of trade with the world, in percent)**

	Value of total trade		Value of exports		Value of imports	
	2010	2019	2010	2019	2010	2019
European Union	31.0	32.2	13.9	11.3	38.6	43.4
WAEMU	12.1	11.6	33.8	30.2	2.4	1.7
United States	1.9	2.3	0.2	3.1	2.7	2.0
South Africa	1.2	0.8	0.0	0.0	1.7	1.2
India	5.2	5.1	10.6	8.3	2.8	3.4
Nigeria	7.2	3.6	0.2	0.6	10.3	5.1
Vietnam	0.9	0.4	0.2	0.6	1.2	0.3
Malaysia	0.2	0.6	0.1	0.1	0.3	0.8
China	6.6	9.4	0.9	6.4	9.2	11.1

Source: Author's calculations, based on IMF Direction of Trade Statistics data.

To sum up, the adoption of the CFA franc as a common currency has had a number of positive macroeconomic effects but has not fostered trade integration among WAEMU countries. The lack of diversification of these countries' exports has led to each of them looking outside the bloc for imports as their economics develop. There is potential for greater trade integration in ECOWAS. However, the potential trade gains that might result from an ECOWAS currency union should not be overstated. As the analysis of WAEMU trade patterns shows, other policies that foster trade integration are needed beyond just the formation of a currency union. This analysis has some important lessons for ECOWAS as it contemplates a currency union.

TOWARD AN AFRICA-WIDE INITIATIVE: THE AFCFTA AGREEMENT IN PERSPECTIVE[5]

In March 2018, African countries signed the AfCFTA agreement, a landmark trade agreement that commits signatory countries to remove tariffs on 90 percent of goods, progressively liberalize trade in services, and address a host of other non-tariff barriers. If successfully implemented, the agreement will create a single African market of over a billion consumers with a total GDP of over US$3 trillion. This will make Africa the largest free trade area in the world.

The AfCFTA has a broad scope, encompassing trade in goods and services, as well as covering investment, intellectual property rights and competition policy, and, possibly, e-commerce. The AfCFTA is complemented by other continental initiatives, including the Protocol on Free Movement of Persons, Right to Residence, and Right to Establishment, and the Single African Air Transport Market (SAATM). The scale of AfCFTA's potential impact makes it vital to understand the main drivers of the agreement and the best methods to harness its opportunities and overcome the risks and challenges. The AfCFTA has been created at a time when the benefits of international trade are being actively contested, and global powers that traditionally promoted trade as a crucial driver of growth are now calling into question its very tenets. This apprehension is not without cause. It is broadly recognized that, while globalization and trade produced the impressive economic expansion of the past three decades, the gains have not been fairly distributed, which raises concerns about the distributed gains of trade among partners. As an outcome, these trade gains are expected to aid in poverty reduction. However, while global poverty has fallen consistent with the Sustainable Development Goals (SDGs), prosperity has not been fully shared and inequality is still wide. Undoubtedly, rising inequality threatens the achievement of the SDG 10—which, therefore, calls for the need to deepen collaboration.

However, given the higher poverty and inequality levels in Africa, can the continent do better with trade? At the global level, Africa's share in world trade has not been impressive over the past two decades. Available data from the World Trade Organization (WTO) suggests that Africa recorded its highest contribution to global trade of 3.48 percent in 2008. Since then, the share has fallen in most years, down to 2.45 percent in 2019. The poor performance of Africa in world trade can be attributed to several factors, including the reliance on primary commodities and natural resources for exports at a time when world trade is largely dominated by manufactured and processed products. According to the 2018 African Trade Report of the African Export-Import Bank, the share of intra-African exports as a percentage of total African exports increased from about 10 percent in 1995 to around 17 percent in 2017, even though this remains low relative to the levels in Europe (69 percent), Asia (59 percent), and North America (31 percent).[6]

For the most part, the AfCFTA has the potential to be a game-changer for stimulating intra-African trade. The agreement leverages on the charter of the tripartite free trade area consisting of the East African Community (EAC), the Southern African Development Community (SADC), and the Common Market for Eastern and Southern Africa (COMESA). The agreement's framework envisages the achievement of broader objectives, including deepening economic integration in Africa consistent with the Agenda 2063. The implementation of the AfCFTA involves a progressive elimination of both tariff and non-tariff barriers to trade in goods in addition to liberalizing trade in services. On the back of this, the AfCFTA aims to create a single and the largest continental market for goods and services.

According to modeling estimations conducted by the UNECA, the AfCFTA is projected to increase the value of intra-African trade by about 15–25 percent (or US$50–US$70 billion) by the year 2040—with the outcome determined by the extent of liberalization efforts—compared to a situation with no AfCFTA in place. From another perspective, the share of intra-African trade would increase by nearly 40 percentage points to over 50 percent, depending on the ambition of the liberalization, in two decades from the start of its implementation in 2020.[7]

Recent evidence compiled by UNECA shows that when African countries trade among themselves, they exchange more manufactured and processed goods, have more knowledge transfer, and create more value. In fact, manufactured goods make up a much higher proportion of regional exports than those leaving the continent. UNCTAD reports that between 2015 and 2017, exports of manufacturing products amounted to 45 percent of intra-African exports. Available estimates reveal that Africa could nearly double its manufacturing output, from US$500 billion to US$930 billion between 2016 and 2025.[8] The real test of the AfCFTA, however, will be how quickly African countries can accelerate export diversification and product sophistication in making trade more inclusive.

Trade diversification of exports is important, as it allows countries to build resilience to contractions in demand, due to economic downturns in importing countries as well as price dips. In the case of commodity-exporting countries, it supports a shift from an over-dependence on raw commodities to higher value–added products and services. Economic diversification allows for more inclusion of small and medium-sized enterprises and helps encourage innovation as more markets open. Given the higher value added on the back of improved innovation, economic diversification enhances overall productivity and turns countries toward a trajectory of increased structural transformation. This is particularly important for Africa, where both productivity and structural transformation are low, relative to other regions in the world.

Between 1990 and 2014, as most fast-growing countries in the world diversified their economies, most African countries instead relied on rents from extractive industries. Except for Rwanda, Senegal, and Sudan, African economies did not diversify their exports. Export diversification for the continent improved only marginally between 1990 and 2014. Recent evidence from IMF export diversification database suggests that Uganda, Tanzania, Mauritius, Malawi, Benin, Burkina Faso, Burundi, and Eritrea are aggressively diversifying their exports. Exports from Central Africa—particularly Chad and Cameroon—are, however, becoming more concentrated. A similar trend is also observed in North Africa, especially in Morocco, where exports are less diversified. In the Southern African region, where countries have diversified their exports to a greater extent, the diversification drive in South Africa is relatively becoming weaker.[9] Against this backdrop, the AfCFTA is expected to enable countries to break into new African markets as they diversify their exports both by destination and types of goods.

The AfCFTA offers particular potential for agricultural products. In 2015, African countries spent about US$63 billion on food imports, largely from outside the continent. UNECA's modeling projects that, by 2040, the AfCFTA will increase intra-African trade in agricultural products by between 20 and 30 percent, with the highest gains in sugar, vegetables, fruit, nuts, beverages, and dairy products.[10] The agreement is expected to expand access to markets at the regional and international levels, thus generating state revenue, increasing farmer income, and expanding both farmer and country capacity to invest in modernizing the agricultural sector through processing and mechanization. As a result, the AfCFTA should stimulate demand for intra-African food imports, supporting a predominantly women-led sector.

Diversification should also lead to increased sophistication of export products. Product sophistication refers to the share of value addition in a product, or product upgrading, which are both associated with increases in productivity and the overall value of exports. Over the past three decades, exports from East Asia have increased in both diversity and quality as a result of integration in regional and global value chains. The quality growth has been especially substantial in manufacturing, although the quality of commodities has also increased, due to the development of vertically integrated industries. On such diversity criteria, African exports have generally lagged behind, and there is no evidence of quality convergence. The AfCFTA will improve export sophistication across the continent by enabling more countries to integrate regional and global value chains and consequently increase the quality of exports. The Pan-African quality infrastructure (PAQI), coupled with a harmonized intellectual policy regime and a whole of Africa competition regime, all foreseen in the AfCFTA, will be critical for diversified, sophisticated, and high-quality regional value chains.

At the regional level, Southern African economies have, on average, the most sophisticated exports. Botswana and South Africa export the most sophisticated goods while Rwanda and Uganda have made the greatest improvements over the past three decades. However, quality improvement of the export basket has been sluggish elsewhere, with some reversals, and there is considerable cross-country heterogeneity within regions. Analysis of sectoral quality shows that some richer and more open countries, such as South Africa and Morocco, have well-established manufacturing exports.

One concern for ECOWAS countries is the lack of growth and diversification of their exports, which might have reached a saturation point without access to a broader set of markets. Like the East Asian economies, they may have reached a saturation point to quality improvement within existing sectors and may need to target new geographic markets that can provide greater scope for growth and innovation to improve their competitive advantage. Other countries, such as Botswana and Mali, have successfully moved up the value chain within their natural resource sectors. In these countries, knowledge transfers to other export sectors can unlock the potential of established or emerging industries.

The argument for new geographical markets, which the AfCFTA offers to ECOWAS, are in line with Hummels and Klenow (2005), Helpman, Melitz, and Rubinstein (2008), Songwe and Winkler (2012), and similar studies, which show clearly that ability to grow exports depends both on extensive margins (gross additions to the export relationships) and intensive margins (survival and persistence of new export relationships). Differences in export performance and product sophistication demonstrate that across the continent, including among the ECOWAS countries, there is potential for increased diversification, the creation of regional vertically integrated industries, and the development of globally competitive regional value chains.

If the AfCFTA is to fulfill its potential in diversifying and transforming African economies in an inclusive manner, however, countries in the region must develop effective policies and strategies for exports, and identify new opportunities for diversification, industrialization, and value chain development. Furthermore, although the AfCFTA can address many important demand-side constraints to trade, particularly those linked to market size, supply-side constraints must also be addressed.

SUMMARY

Promoting deeper trade integration has taken center stage in recent discussions at the policy level in Africa. For the most part, the design and framework of the AfCFTA potentially embody a "win-win" approach such that all countries across Africa and vulnerable communities within these countries benefit from the agreement. However, in order to achieve this, the AfCFTA will require accompanying policies and a strong focus on achieving tangible outcomes from its sister initiative, the Boosting Intra-African Trade (BIAT) Action Plan.

BIAT, which forms part of the broader initiatives toward the Agenda 2063, offers a framework for addressing key constraints to intra-Africa trade and diversification under seven clusters: trade policy, trade facilitation, productive capacity, trade-related infrastructure, trade finance, trade information, and factor market integration. Particular attention should be given to trade facilitation and building productive capacities. Trade facilitation is key to reducing non-tariff trade costs, and is important for ensuring inclusive benefits, since landlocked countries and small, informal, and female traders are usually more burdened by inadequate trade facilitation. In addition, given that the implementation of the AfCFTA may be associated with trade creation, building productive capacities through re-skilling job-training programs will be crucial to ensuring that displaced workers and vulnerable persons are able to participate in welfare-enhancing opportunities under the AfCFTA. In particular, Africans must be equipped with the skills needed to engage in skill-intensive manufacturing industries such as apparel and machinery. This is critical, since manufactured products are increasingly dominating global trade.

While the AfCFTA aims to progressively eliminate tariffs, concerted collaborative efforts are needed at the policy level to address the non-tariff barriers to trade. It is important to note that the poor trade logistics and infrastructural deficit should be a major priority for countries in order to foster deeper integration. Even though both the shares of intra-RTA and intra-regional trade have marginally improved in the past decade, the question that faces ECOWAS policymakers is how they will best grasp the opportunity offered by the AfCFTA and what policy frameworks—including fiscal, monetary, and exchange rate regimes—will help them achieve the goal of deepening trade integration.

4

Macroeconomic and Structural Convergence

A central issue for the stability and prosperity of currency unions is that members agree on and attain similar macroeconomic conjunctures. The ECOWAS region has reached agreement on a set of criteria—four main indicators and two ancillary ones—to evaluate macroeconomic convergence among the prospective members of the union. This chapter provides an evaluation of progress toward meeting those criteria and provides a critical evaluation of whether the criteria that have been identified are adequate to ensure a resilient monetary union. The chapter then analyzes the proposed ECOWAS currency union from the perspective of the analytical considerations discussed in chapter 2. Appendix B provides a comparative listing of macroeconomic convergence and performance indicators in all existing currency unions.

It is worth reiterating that the convergence indicators discussed below should be understood and interpreted from the perspective of the fundamental objectives of promoting growth and stability. A currency union, and the conditions for it to work well, should not be seen as ends in themselves, although they might serve as a useful organizing framework for achieving the underlying objectives.

EVALUATING PROGRESS ON
MACROECONOMIC CONVERGENCE

The four primary macroeconomic convergence criteria agreed upon by ECOWAS governments are as follows:

- Budget deficit to GDP ratio ≤ 3%

- Average annual inflation rate ≤ 10% (and ≤ 5% by 2019)

- Central bank financing of the budget deficit ≤ 10% previous year's tax revenue

- Gross external reserves ≥ 3 months of imports

The two secondary convergence criteria are:

- Ratio of total public debt to GDP ≤ 70%

- Nominal exchange rate variation ± 10%

Progress on meeting the convergence criteria has been mixed. The 2018 ECOWAS Macroeconomic Convergence Report points out that no country met all six convergence criteria in 2018, compared to three countries in 2017 and one in 2016. The deterioration of macroeconomic convergence in 2018 was mainly caused by the challenges in meeting the budget deficit criterion. Five countries met the criterion in 2018, down from seven in 2017 but higher than three in 2016. The performance on the other three primary criteria regarding inflation, central bank financing of budget deficit, and reserves slightly improved in 2018, with twelve, fourteen, and fourteen countries in compliance, respectively. Putting all of this together, two countries met all four primary criteria in 2018 against four in 2017 and one in 2016. Eleven countries met the two secondary criteria in 2018, compared to ten countries in 2017 and eight in 2016.

There are significant risks to moving forward with a monetary union if the agreed-upon criteria are not met by all countries. This could reduce the credibility of the currency zone and would, at the outset, undermine the enforcement mechanisms that are meant to ensure consistency of economic policies across member countries.

A different approach would be to consider the case for convergence based on trade-offs among different criteria. For instance, Nigeria's low level of public debt (28 percent of GDP, well below the threshold of 70 percent of

GDP) could be seen as offsetting its high inflation rate and exchange rate volatility. This approach carries significant risks as well, since the commitment of ECOWAS members to specific criteria could come into question, especially at times of macroeconomic and financial stress, potentially exacerbating those stresses.

EXTERNAL VULNERABILITY INDICATORS

The criteria that have been identified as indicators of macroeconomic convergence are indeed crucial. However, as the world economy becomes more interconnected through trade and financial linkages, the potential vulnerability of ECOWAS member countries to external demand shocks and external financing shocks should be a key consideration as well. The COVID-19 pandemic, which dampened global demand for exports and led to a pullback of capital from emerging and developing economies, drives home these vulnerabilities.

Consider a few examples. First, the contribution of net exports to GDP growth is an indicator of a country's reliance on foreign rather than domestic demand for growth. It is, thus, an indicator of a country's sensitivity to global demand and business cycle conditions. Second, current account deficits also need to be taken into account, since they have implications for sensitivity to global financial conditions. Countries with larger current account deficits, which rely more on external financing, are more susceptible to changes in advanced economy monetary policy stances, global financial conditions, and volatile investor sentiment (these external factors are interrelated with one another, of course). Third, new measures of reserve adequacy tend to focus more on capital account rather than current account vulnerability. In particular, given the role of high levels of foreign currency–denominated external debt in precipitating many previous emerging market balance of payments crises, it is important to consider the ratio of reserves to external debt rather than just reserve coverage of three months of imports.[1]

A brief review of the external vulnerability positions of ECOWAS countries presents some grounds for concern (see table 4-1). In 2018, eleven countries' ratios of exports of goods and services to GDP were higher than 20 percent. In principle, this could be a healthy sign of these countries' competitiveness in global markets. On the other hand, it also signals a high level of export dependency, particularly since commodities constitute a significant share of these exports. In conjunction with the low level of intra-ECOWAS trade, this implies the vulnerability of many of these economies to commodity price shocks and fluctuations in global demand conditions.

In 2019, according to IMF estimates (as of April 2020), twelve of fifteen ECOWAS countries had significant current account deficits of at least 3 percent of GDP. Nigeria had a current account surplus in 2018, but this swung to a nearly 4 percent of GDP deficit in 2019. Consequently, the overall external financing needs of the ECOWAS group increased to 4.3 percent of the group's total GDP in 2019. These figures highlight the region's vulnerability to external financing shocks, which could be precipitated by global financial market conditions and other related factors.

As discussed above, the adequacy of international reserves is another area where traditional metrics are important but might not be sufficient to protect against external vulnerability. In 2019, thirteen of the fifteen countries met the criterion that gross reserves should be sufficient to finance at least three months of imports. However, the ratio of reserves to external debt was below 100 percent for the eight WAEMU countries based on their overall reserves, and this was also the case for each of the other ECOWAS economies, raising the risk of balance of payment crises in the event of sudden stops or reversals of capital flows that could be triggered by global financial market conditions.[2] In fact, for all countries except Nigeria, this ratio was below 40 percent in 2019, heightening rollover and repayment risks if global financing conditions were to tighten sharply.

CO-MOVEMENT

One important criterion in determining the optimality of a currency zone is whether countries in the proposed zone are subject to similar shocks. A simplistic, first-pass approach to this issue is to examine the co-movement of key macroeconomic variables—in particular, GDP growth and inflation—across the countries. While cross-country correlations of these variables do not, by themselves, reveal the nature of the underlying macroeconomic shocks buffeting these economies, they do provide a benchmark for evaluating how common or different the exposure of the countries might be to such shocks.

Table 4-2 shows the bivariate correlations of annual GDP growth among the ECOWAS countries over the period 2009–17. One feature that is immediately apparent is that, while there are a handful of high bivariate correlations, the average correlations between GDP growth in any given country

TABLE 4-1. Indicators of Macroeconomic Convergence and External Vulnerability

Country	Primary balance Ratio to GDP (percent)		Public debt Ratio to GDP (percent)		Exports of goods and services Ratio to GDP (percent)	Current account Ratio to GDP (percent)	Reserves (USD billion)	External debt Ratio to GDP (percent)	Reserves to external debt (percent)
	2009–2019	2019	2009–2019	2019	2018	2019	2019	2019	2019
Benin*	-1.6	-0.4	28.2	40.9	16.3	-5.1	–	22.8	–
Burkina Faso*	-3.1	-1.7	34.0	42.9	30.7	-4.4	–	22.4	–
Cabo Verde	-4.1	0.5	105.0	123.5	49.1	-0.2	0.7	98.7	37.1
Côte d'Ivoire*	-1.4	-1.0	52.8	52.7	29.8	-2.7	–	26.6	–
The Gambia	-0.9	-0.3	65.0	80.9	19.3	-5.4	0.2	45.1	29.1
Ghana	-2.6	-1.4	46.8	63.8	35.0	-2.7	7.1	30.2	35.2
Guinea	-2.4	-1.8	44.8	45.4	33.1	-13.7	1.2	19.3	47.6
Guinea Bissau*	-1.8	-3.7	70.0	69.2	25.9	-10.2	–	23.9	–
Liberia	-3.3	-4.9	35.0	45.5	57.1	-22.3	0.5	36.2	45.2
Mali*	-2.3	-2.0	29.8	37.6	23.6	-4.2	–	26.3	–
Niger*	-3.9	-2.8	35.5	55.8	15.6	-13.2	–	25.3	–
Nigeria	-2.2	-3.4	19.6	29.8	17.1	-3.8	39.0	15.5	56.4
Senegal*	-2.4	-1.0	43.6	63.3	21.8	-9.1	–	47.1	–
Sierra Leone	-3.2	-0.6	48.0	64.5	25.3	-13.9	0.5	39.7	31.7
Togo*	-3.0	-0.2	65.5	72.6	31.7	-4.3	–	23.5	–

Data sources: Primary balance, public debt, and current account data are from October 2019 IMF World Economic Outlook. External debt data are from April 2020 IMF Sub-Saharan Africa Regional Economic Outlook. Exports and reserves data are from the IMF International Financial Statistics.

Notes: Asterisks indicate members of WAEMU. Total reserves for WAEMU countries stood at USD 15.8 billion in 2019 and total external debt at 28.8 percent of GDP, according to the IMF. Reserves amounted to roughly 41.9 percent of WAEMU external debt.

and GDP growth in the other ECOWAS countries are quite low. The average correlations are close to 0.2 for Burkina Faso, Guinea, and Niger, but much smaller (and, in some cases, even negative) for the remaining countries. These correlations indicate little business cycle co-movement among the ECOWAS countries.

Table 4-3 repeats this exercise, but this time limited to the WAEMU countries. The average correlations are somewhat higher, but, even among this smaller group of countries that are part of a long-standing currency union, the degree of business cycle co-movement is quite modest.

In addition to looking at GDP growth, co-movement of inflation can also provide some hints about the commonality of shocks hitting different countries within the proposed currency zone. Table 4-4 shows the bivariate correlations of annual CPI inflation among ECOWAS countries over the period 2009–17. It is interesting to note that there are a number of high bivariate inflation correlations. The average bivariate correlations for each country with the other ECOWAS countries are also higher, with eight

TABLE 4-2. ECOWAS: Bivariate Correlations of GDP Growth

	Benin*	Burkina Faso*	Cabo Verde	Côte d'Ivoire*	The Gambia	Ghana	Guinea
Benin*	1.00						
Burkina Faso*	−0.02	1.00					
Cabo Verde	0.06	0.58	1.00				
Côte d'Ivoire*	0.55	−0.28	−0.25	1.00			
The Gambia	−0.09	−0.08	−0.62	0.50	1.00		
Ghana	−0.09	0.55	0.32	−0.66	−0.47	1.00	
Guinea	0.32	0.67	0.85	0.13	−0.41	0.28	1.00
Guinea Bissau*	−0.44	0.17	0.55	−0.66	−0.50	0.23	0.10
Liberia	0.11	0.37	−0.21	−0.32	0.11	0.76	−0.11
Mali*	−0.20	−0.27	0.07	−0.06	−0.13	−0.60	−0.17
Niger*	0.34	0.52	0.03	0.46	0.23	0.09	0.52
Nigeria	−0.25	0.10	−0.62	−0.39	0.32	0.26	−0.59
Senegal*	0.08	0.08	0.38	0.62	0.22	−0.61	0.50
Sierra Leone	0.63	0.39	0.06	0.03	0.02	0.39	0.21
Togo*	0.72	0.08	0.17	0.62	−0.14	0.05	0.55
Average	0.12	0.20	0.10	0.02	−0.07	0.04	0.20

countries having averages of 0.25 or higher. Table 4-5 shows that bivariate inflation correlations are even higher among the WAEMU countries, with most countries having average correlations in the 0.4–0.6 range. Thus, the co-movement of inflation in ECOWAS and WAEMU is much stronger than respective measures of co-movement in GDP fluctuations in the two areas.

PRINCIPAL COMPONENT ANALYSIS

Bivariate correlations constitute a coarse measure and can sometimes be difficult to interpret as a summary measure of co-movement among multiple countries. A more formal approach is to use a principal components analysis to evaluate the degree of cross-country co-movement in a particular variable. This procedure provides a way of assessing if there is a principal component—essentially, a linear combination constructed using that variable for each country—that can explain a significant fraction of the variance of that variable across all the countries in the sample. The greater the vari-

Guinea Bissau*	Liberia	Mali*	Niger*	Nigeria	Senegal*	Sierra Leone	Togo*
1.00							
−0.17	1.00						
0.43	−0.78	1.00					
−0.66	0.16	−0.38	1.00				
−0.16	0.54	−0.04	0.06	1.00			
−0.02	−0.69	0.33	0.25	−0.68	1.00		
−0.35	0.62	−0.58	0.32	0.13	−0.36	1.00	
−0.40	0.09	−0.42	0.55	−0.44	0.27	0.28	1.00
−0.13	0.03	−0.20	0.18	−0.13	0.03	0.13	0.14

Notes: Asterisks indicate WAEMU countries. Correlations are based on annual real GDP growth rates for 2009–2017. The row "Average" indicates average bivariate correlations of GDP growth in the relevant country (in the column heading) with GDP growth in each of the other fourteen ECOWAS countries.

ance contribution is of that principal component (usually referred to as the first principal component), the greater the degree of co-movement of that variable across countries.

Table 4-6 shows the results of principal component analysis on GDP growth and inflation for ECOWAS and WAEMU. The first principal component explains about 28 percent of GDP growth variance among ECOWAS countries over the period 2009–17. This proportion rises to 43 percent for the WAEMU countries. Inflation co-movement is even higher for both groups of countries, and the first principal component accounts for nearly half of the variance of inflation in both groups. This confirms the earlier result that inflation co-movement is higher than GDP co-movement.

One interpretation of the weak GDP growth co-movement and strong inflation co-movement in the ECOWAS region is that inflation in these countries is driven more by common disturbances, which could be global commodity price shocks or global demand shocks. By contrast, the shocks to demand and/or supply that drive GDP growth fluctuations are more specific to each country. Validation of such statements would, of course, require more careful econometric work to disentangle demand and supply shocks, as well as domestic and external shocks.

The second panel of table 4-6 adds one other perspective—whether the degree of co-movement has changed over time. It is interesting to note that there is a sharp increase in GDP co-movement among WAEMU countries in the last eight years relative to a longer period (2001–17). By contrast, CPI inflation co-movement in WAEMU is lower in the last eight years relative to the longer period analyzed in the second panel (52 percent variance contribution of the first principal component versus 75 percent). This probably reflects the sharp and synchronized spike in inflation in all WAEMU countries in 2008. Among the ECOWAS countries, GDP growth co-movement in the recent sample is slightly higher than over the full period (28 percent versus 22 percent), while inflation co-movement is basically the same.

The results of the principal components analysis confirm the results based on correlations that there is limited co-movement of GDP growth among ECOWAS countries, although the increase in correlations of GDP growth among WAEMU countries also reveals the potential endogeneity of this measure. A currency union might foster increased trade and other forms of economic integration that lead to greater synchronization of output fluctuations.

TABLE 4-3. WAEMU: Bivariate Correlations of GDP Growth

	Benin	Burkina Faso	Côte d'Ivoire	Guinea Bissau	Mali	Niger	Senegal	Togo
Benin	1.00							
Burkina Faso	-0.02	1.00						
Côte d'Ivoire	0.55	-0.28	1.00					
Guinea Bissau	-0.44	0.17	-0.66	1.00				
Mali	-0.20	-0.27	-0.06	0.43	1.00			
Niger	0.34	0.52	0.46	-0.66	-0.38	1.00		
Senegal	0.08	0.08	0.62	-0.02	0.33	0.25	1.00	
Togo	0.72	0.08	0.62	-0.40	-0.42	0.55	0.27	1.00
Average	0.15	0.04	0.18	-0.23	-0.08	0.15	0.23	0.20

Notes: Correlations are based on annual GDP growth rates for 2009–2017. The row "Average" indicates average bivariate correlations of GDP growth in the relevant country (in the column heading) with GDP growth in each of the other seven WAEMU countries.

TABLE 4-4. ECOWAS: Bivariate Correlations of Inflation

	Benin*	Burkina Faso*	Cabo Verde	Côte d'Ivoire*	The Gambia	Ghana	Guinea
Benin*	1.00						
Burkina Faso*	0.82	1.00					
Cabo Verde	0.70	0.64	1.00				
Côte d'Ivoire*	0.29	0.45	0.81	1.00			
The Gambia	−0.42	−0.29	−0.63	−0.43	1.00		
Ghana	−0.80	−0.50	−0.88	−0.50	0.60	1.00	
Guinea	0.59	0.46	0.83	0.77	−0.47	−0.76	1.00
Guinea Bissau*	0.48	0.57	0.58	0.69	0.12	−0.43	0.71
Liberia	−0.26	−0.10	−0.26	−0.18	0.80	0.25	−0.24
Mali*	0.78	0.77	0.67	0.26	−0.62	−0.62	0.46
Niger*	−0.02	0.42	0.23	0.42	−0.23	0.10	−0.16
Nigeria	0.17	0.01	−0.12	−0.25	0.38	−0.13	−0.14
Senegal*	0.52	0.47	0.58	0.64	0.11	−0.54	0.77
Sierra Leone	0.55	0.34	0.66	0.48	−0.04	−0.75	0.69
Togo*	0.42	0.58	0.66	0.59	−0.72	−0.44	0.30
Average	0.27	0.33	0.32	0.29	−0.13	−0.38	0.27

Guinea Bissau*	Liberia	Mali*	Niger*	Nigeria	Senegal*	Sierra Leone	Togo*
1.00							
0.20	1.00						
0.20	−0.41	1.00					
0.05	−0.07	0.14	1.00				
0.24	0.38	−0.18	−0.13	1.00			
0.96	0.21	0.13	−0.12	0.28	1.00		
0.75	0.21	0.25	−0.21	0.54	0.82	1.00	
0.19	−0.54	0.62	0.71	−0.10	0.05	0.16	1.00
0.38	0.00	0.18	0.08	0.07	0.35	0.32	0.18

Notes: Asterisks indicate WAEMU countries. Correlations are based on annual CPI inflation for 2009–2017. The row "Average" indicates average bivariate correlations of inflation in the relevant country (in the column heading) with inflation in each of the other fourteen ECOWAS countries.

TABLE 4-5. WAEMU: Bivariate Correlations of Inflation

	Benin	Burkina Faso	Côte d'Ivoire	Guinea Bissau	Mali	Niger	Senegal	Togo
Benin	1.00							
Burkina Faso	0.82	1.00						
Côte d'Ivoire	0.29	0.45	1.00					
Guinea Bissau	0.48	0.57	0.69	1.00				
Mali	0.78	0.77	0.26	0.20	1.00			
Niger	-0.02	0.42	0.42	0.05	0.14	1.00		
Senegal	0.52	0.47	0.64	0.96	0.13	-0.12	1.00	
Togo	0.42	0.58	0.59	0.19	0.62	0.71	0.05	1.00
Average	0.47	0.58	0.48	0.45	0.41	0.23	0.38	0.45

Notes: Correlations are based on annual CPI inflation for 2009–2017. The row "Average" indicates average bivariate correlations of inflation in the relevant country (in the column heading) with inflation in each of the other seven WAEMU countries.

TABLE 4-6. **Principal Components Analysis**
of GDP Growth and CPI Inflation

	Variance Contributions of First Principal Component (in percent)			
	2009–2017		2001–2017	
	GDP growth	CPI inflation	GDP growth	CPI inflation
ECOWAS	27.7	47.1	21.7	48.2
WAEMU	43.2	51.8	25.6	74.9

Notes: The numbers in this table reflect the degree of contemporaneous co-movement of the relevant variable across countries.

ECONOMIC STRUCTURE AND DIVERSIFICATION

Another aspect related to the suitability of a group of countries for entering a currency union is the similarity in their economic structures as well as their extent of diversification. Countries with similar economic structures are less likely to face asymmetric shocks, which would make it easier for them to use common monetary policy settings as implied by a currency union. More diversified economies are also better able to withstand external and industry-specific shocks.

Table 4-7 presents some basic data, at a very broad level of disaggregation, on the economic structures of ECOWAS countries using sectoral GDP shares computed on a value-added basis. The share of the primary sector in GDP averages 32 percent in ECOWAS (unweighted average), ranging from 7 percent in Cabo Verde to 40 percent or more in Guinea, Liberia, Mali, Niger, Sierra Leone, and Togo. The average share of the primary sector in GDP is 31 percent for WAEMU countries and 34 percent for non-WAEMU countries. Industry—a category that includes manufacturing and construction— accounts on average for 21 percent of value added in ECOWAS economies. A further breakdown of industry (not shown here) revealed that the manufacturing sector by itself accounts for at most 12 percent of any ECOWAS economy (the sole exception is Senegal, where the share is 17 percent). Thus, the ECOWAS economies are all well short of the industrial takeoff stage and remain significantly reliant on the primary sector, including agriculture and resource extraction, for their output.

This table reveals two important aspects of ECOWAS economies that are relevant considerations for the advisability of a currency union as well as the suitability of alternative exchange rate regimes. First, there are considerable differences among ECOWAS economies in terms of their economic structures. Second, these economies are not well diversified and retain a high degree of reliance on the primary sector for generating GDP.

These themes are also evident in an examination of the structure of exports. Exports of agricultural products, raw materials, and commodities account for the overwhelming share of merchandise exports for ECOWAS economies. Nigeria's oil exports represent about 96 percent of its merchandise exports, with manufactured goods representing only 1 percent. Manufactures represent only 15 percent of Ghana's exports, while the average for WAEMU countries is 24 percent. Thus, the ECOWAS region as a whole has a relatively undiversified structure of exports, with a heavy reliance on agriculture, energy, and other commodities. This leaves the region vulnerable to commodity price fluctuations, which tend to be volatile and highly persistent.

The lack of diversification of ECOWAS countries' exports can be further illustrated using export diversification indexes constructed by the IMF.[3] These indexes are shown in the last three columns of table 4-7. The overall export diversification index captures the degree of diversification of a country's exports across products as well as trading partners, with a higher value of the index implying less diversification. The average of the overall diversification index for ECOWAS countries in 2014 (the latest year for which these data are available) was 4.3, compared to the world average of 3.6. The corresponding averages for advanced economies and emerging markets are 2.4 and 3.8, respectively.

The low level of diversification of ECOWAS exports is both at the extensive margin (the number of export products or trading partners) and the intensive margin (the shares of export volumes across active products or trading partners). For the former, the ECOWAS average is 0.6, compared to the world average of 0.3 (0.1 for advanced economies; 0.4 for emerging markets). For the latter, the ECOWAS average is 3.7, compared to the world average of 3.2 (2.2 for advanced economies; 3.4 for emerging markets).

Thus, the averages for ECOWAS, WAEMU, and non-WAEMU countries all show substantially less diversification than corresponding global aver-

TABLE 4-7. Components of GDP and Structure of Exports

| Country | GDP composition (shares, in percent) | | | Structure of exports | | | | | | Export Diversification Indexes | | |
| | | | | Merchandise exports (percent of total merchandise exports) | | | | Total exports (percent of total exports) | | | | |
	Primary	Industry	Services	Agriculture and raw materials	Food exports	Other Commodities Exports	Manufacture Exports	Merchandise Exports	Service Exports	Overall Exports	Extensive Margin	Intensive Margin
Benin*	25.1	23.5	51.3	50.0	33.4	2.4	14.2	84.8	15.2	3.55	0.79	2.76
Burkina Faso*	31.5	20.2	48.3	44.0	33.4	10.7	11.7	84.4	15.6	3.77	0.60	3.17
Cabo Verde	7.1	21.4	71.5	0.0	83.6	0.0	16.4	9.7	90.3	4.48	0.24	4.25
Côte d'Ivoire*	23.7	27.1	49.3	–	–	–	–	93.2	6.8	4.13	0.69	3.44
The Gambia	28.5	16.0	55.5	9.5	66.4	1.6	22.6	40.8	59.2	3.99	0.06	3.93
Ghana	21.3	33.3	45.3	8.5	51.3	25.4	14.8	64.0	36.0	4.18	0.07	4.11
Guinea	52.2	13.4	34.5	–	–	–	–	93.1	6.9	4.86	0.33	4.53
Guinea Bissau*	18.3	36.2	45.5	–	–	–	–	97.9	2.1	5.24	0.15	5.10
Liberia	45.0	12.4	42.7	–	–	–	–	92.1	7.9	4.83	2.16	2.68
Mali*	41.2	19.5	39.3	38.9	38.3	0.6	21.8	85.3	14.7	4.16	0.64	3.52
Niger*	42.0	16.8	41.2	1.1	38.8	50.7	9.4	84.9	15.1	5.21	0.02	5.19
Nigeria	21.1	22.5	56.4	0.2	2.0	96.5	1.1	91.5	8.5	5.62	0.78	4.84
Senegal*	19.9	28.1	51.9	2.2	36.8	19.9	36.5	64.4	35.6	2.99	0.68	2.31
Sierra Leone	61.6	5.3	33.1	1.0	78.0	0.5	20.4	67.5	32.5	4.96	1.96	3.00
Togo*	47.0	19.2	33.9	9.5	22.5	16.7	51.3	67.4	32.6	2.55	0.37	2.19
Averages												
ECOWAS	32.4	21.0	46.7	15.0	44.0	20.4	20.0	74.7	25.3	4.3	0.6	3.7
WAEMU	31.1	23.8	45.1	24.3	33.9	16.8	24.2	82.8	17.2	3.9	0.5	3.5
Non-WAEMU	33.8	17.8	48.4	3.8	56.2	24.8	15.1	65.5	34.5	4.7	0.8	3.9

Data sources: GDP composition and export structure data are from WB World Development Index, 2017. Export Index data are from the IMF, 2014.

Notes: Primary includes forestry, hunting, and fishing, as well as cultivation of crops and livestock production. Industry includes mining, manufacturing, construction, electricity, water, and gas. Services include wholesale and retail trade, transport, and government, financial, professional, and personal services such as education, health care, and real estate services. Asterisks indicate members of WAEMU. Lower Export Diversification Index values indicate higher diversification. Extensive margin reflects the number of export products or trading partners. Intensive margin reflects the shares of export volumes across active products or trading partners. The averages shown in the last three rows are unweighted averages for the relevant country groups.

ages or overall averages for emerging markets/developing countries in other regions.

SOURCES AND SYMMETRY OF SHOCKS[4]

This section evaluates the sources of macroeconomic fluctuations in ECOWAS using simple vector autoregression (VAR) models. The objective of this exercise is to gauge the relative importance of domestic versus external shocks in driving fluctuations in output growth and inflation, as well as to shed light on which external shocks are most relevant. The findings have potential implications for the design of the exchange rate regime. This exercise is intended to be mainly suggestive, as the lack of high-frequency data over a long time span makes it difficult to estimate dynamic models with sophisticated identification schemes and dynamic structures.

This exercise is based on a simple nonstructural or reduced-form panel vector autoregression (PVAR) approach, as proposed by Holtz-Eakin and others (1988). This approach can capture the heterogeneities in interdependent economies and does so with minimal a priori structure imposed on the model, but at the cost of having to evaluate the relative importance of different shocks through different models rather than in one comprehensive model that nests multiple sources of shocks. Appendix B contains more details about the econometric model, the macroeconomic variables used in the analysis, and a description of the data and relevant sources. It is worth emphasizing up front that the data used for the exercise are annual, cover the period 2009–16, and were available for only six of the fifteen ECOWAS countries (Côte d'Ivoire, Ghana, Nigeria, Sierra Leone, the Gambia, and Togo), of which three are part of WAEMU.[5]

In view of the extensive literature on the importance of terms-of-trade shocks in driving economic fluctuations in developing economies (see discussion below), particularly commodity exporters, we begin with a focus on that source of external shocks. Given the paucity of data, only small-dimensional models were used in this exercise. We first estimated three-variable VARs—with GDP growth, CPI inflation, and changes in the terms of trade—for (1) the full set of ECOWAS countries, (2) WAEMU, and (3) non-WAEMU countries in ECOWAS.

The results from these simple PVAR models suggest that a positive shock to changes in the terms of trade enhances the GDP growth of non-WAEMU countries and reduces their CPI inflation for about three years. For a com-

modity exporter such as Nigeria, a positive terms-of-trade shock is beneficial on both counts. For WAEMU countries, by contrast, a similar positive
terms-of-trade shock has a small negative effect on growth and a positive
effect on inflation for about three years. One possible reason is that a terms-
of-trade shock, which often has the characteristics of a supply shock, tends
to appreciate the real exchange rate. Measures to keep the nominal exchange
rate stable might therefore lead to real exchange rate adjustment taking
place through domestic inflation. This, in turn, might induce tightening of
monetary policy to control inflation, reducing economic activity.[6]

The marked difference in GDP growth and inflation responses of
WAEMU versus non-WAEMU countries points to potential complications
in using a consistent monetary policy setting for all ECOWAS countries.
This point is highlighted by the fact that the average ECOWAS GDP growth
and inflation responses to an innovation in the changes in the terms of trade
is essentially zero, despite the large effects on these variables within sub-
groups of ECOWAS countries.

An analysis of the data shows that fluctuations in the terms of trade are
highly persistent. From a statistical perspective, using changes in the terms
of trade ensures stationary data. However, this could mask some of the
effects of shocks to variables that are stationary but have highly persistent
fluctuations. Hence, it is also worth considering alternative models using
levels of the terms of trade. Table 4-8 shows the results of forecast error
variance decompositions from three-variable models with GDP growth,
CPI inflation, and the terms of trade.[7] The variance decompositions are a
measure of the relative importance of different shocks over various time
horizons.

Panel A shows results from panel VARs estimated using data for all
ECOWAS countries for which data were available. At short forecast horizons, neither inflation shocks nor terms-of-trade shocks account for GDP
growth fluctuations. Even at medium-term horizons (three to five years),
neither of those shocks contributes much. At longer horizons, terms of trade
become more important, accounting for 28 percent of GDP growth fluctuations. The variance decompositions for inflation show that terms-of-trade
shocks account for one-third of CPI inflation over the medium term, with
the share rising to 38 percent over the long term. In other words, even if
terms-of-trade shocks are an important driver of GDP growth fluctuations
among ECOWAS countries only at long-term horizons, these shocks are important for fluctuations in CPI inflation even in the medium term.

TABLE 4-8. Variance Decompositions: VARs with GDP Growth, Inflation, Terms of Trade

A. ECOWAS

Forecast horizon	GDP growth: sources of fluctutation			CPI Inflation: Sources of Fluctuation		
	GDP growth	CPI inflation	Terms of trade	GDP growth	CPI inflation	Terms of trade
0	0.00	0.00	0	0.00	0.00	0.00
1	1.00	0.00	0	0.04	0.96	0.00
2	0.95	0.05	0	0.09	0.81	0.10
3	0.92	0.08	0	0.14	0.65	0.21
4	0.88	0.11	0.01	0.19	0.52	0.29
5	0.84	0.13	0.03	0.22	0.45	0.33
6	0.78	0.16	0.06	0.25	0.40	0.35
7	0.70	0.19	0.11	0.26	0.38	0.37
8	0.61	0.22	0.17	0.27	0.36	0.37
9	0.52	0.25	0.23	0.27	0.35	0.38
10	0.44	0.28	0.28	0.27	0.35	0.38

B. WAEMU

Forecast horizon	GDP growth: sources of fluctutation			CPI Inflation: Sources of Fluctuation		
	GDP growth	CPI inflation	Terms of trade	GDP growth	CPI inflation	Terms of trade
0	0.00	0.00	0.00	0.00	0.00	0.00
1	1.00	0.00	0.00	0.02	0.98	0.00
2	0.80	0.00	0.20	0.09	0.89	0.03
3	0.64	0.00	0.35	0.12	0.78	0.10
4	0.54	0.01	0.45	0.14	0.68	0.18
5	0.47	0.01	0.52	0.16	0.58	0.26
6	0.42	0.01	0.57	0.18	0.49	0.33
7	0.38	0.02	0.60	0.19	0.41	0.39
8	0.36	0.02	0.63	0.21	0.34	0.45
9	0.34	0.02	0.65	0.22	0.29	0.50
10	0.32	0.02	0.66	0.23	0.23	0.54

c. Non-WAEMU (Ghana, Nigeria, The Gambia)

Forecast horizon	GDP growth: sources of fluctutation			CPI Inflation: Sources of Fluctuation		
	GDP growth	CPI inflation	Terms of trade	GDP growth	CPI inflation	Terms of trade
0	0.00	0.00	0.00	0.00	0.00	0.00
1	1.00	0.00	0.00	0.11	0.89	0.00
2	0.89	0.11	0.00	0.11	0.75	0.13
3	0.77	0.19	0.04	0.14	0.63	0.23
4	0.63	0.27	0.10	0.16	0.56	0.28
5	0.50	0.33	0.17	0.18	0.52	0.30
6	0.39	0.38	0.23	0.19	0.49	0.32
7	0.32	0.41	0.27	0.19	0.48	0.32
8	0.27	0.44	0.29	0.20	0.48	0.33
9	0.24	0.45	0.31	0.20	0.47	0.33
10	0.22	0.46	0.32	0.20	0.47	0.33

Notes: This table shows forecast error variance decompositions from three-variable VARs (GDP growth, CPI inflation, and the terms of trade). The numbers shown are shares of total forecast error variance at different forecast horizons attributable to shocks to different variables in the model. See appendix D for details about the econometric specifications and data.

Panel B shows that, when similar models are estimated just for WAEMU countries, terms-of-trade shocks are even more important for GDP growth fluctuations. The variance contribution of these shocks is about 50 percent over the medium term, rising to 66 percent over the long term. These shocks account for about a quarter of fluctuations in inflation over the medium term, with this share rising to more than half over the long term. Panel C shows that, for the non-WAEMU countries, terms-of-trade shocks account for about one-third of the fluctuations in inflation over the medium and long terms.

We also estimated similar models using other external shocks, such as world GDP growth, the world interest rate (proxied by U.S. short-term interest rates), and uncertainty in global financial markets (proxied by the VIX). All of these models showed that, while other external shocks do have some explanatory power for GDP growth and inflation fluctuations in ECOWAS, they are far less important than terms-of-trade shocks.

The results above should be interpreted with caution, given the limited time span of the data and concerns about its quality, in addition to the reduced-form nature of the estimation exercise. Nevertheless, the findings above are consistent with the conclusion of a large body of existing literature that, for small open economies, shocks to the terms of trade are a key driver of economic fluctuations.[8] More important, the results show that, for ECOWAS countries, terms-of-trade shocks are a key driver of fluctuations in inflation. For a putative currency union that will have a common monetary policy stance for all member countries, a key issue, then, is the degree of symmetry of terms-of-trade shocks hitting the countries in the union.

Table 4-9 reports correlations of different measures of the terms of trade for the two major economies in ECOWAS—Nigeria and Ghana—and WAEMU. The terms of trade for WAEMU are calculated as a simple average of the terms of trade for the constituent countries (WAEMU [1]) and also by weighting each country by its nominal GDP (WAEMU [2]). Panel A shows the pairwise correlations of levels (first four columns) and changes (last four columns) in the terms of trade. Based on either measure, Nigeria's terms of trade are strongly positively correlated with Ghana's terms of trade. However, the terms of trade for Nigeria are negatively correlated with those of WAEMU, whether the latter is calculated as an unweighted or weighted measure. Ghana's terms of trade are weakly positively correlated with those of WAEMU. This configuration of correlations suggests some difficulties in using a common monetary policy setting for ECOWAS.

TABLE 4-9. Cross-Country Correlations of ECOWAS Countries' Terms of Trade

PANEL A. Levels of and Changes in Terms of Trade

	Levels				Changes			
	(1)	(2)	(3)	(4)	(1)	(2)	(3)	(4)
(1) Nigeria	1.00				1.00			
(2) Ghana	0.55	1.00			0.40	1.00		
(3) WAEMU [1]	−0.41	0.35	1.00		−0.27	0.24	1.00	
(4) WAEMU [2]	−0.13	0.62	0.90	1.00	−0.24	0.41	0.85	1.00

PANEL B. Residuals from Univariate AR Models

	AR(1) Model				AR(2) Model			
	(1)	(2)	(3)	(4)	(1)	(2)	(3)	(4)
(1) Nigeria	1.00				1.00			
(2) Ghana	0.47	1.00			0.44	1.00		
(3) WAEMU [1]	−0.34	0.23	1.00		−0.11	0.38	1.00	
(4) WAEMU [2]	−0.34	0.33	0.88	1.00	−0.06	0.51	0.70	1.00

Notes: The table shows the bivariate correlations for the annual terms of trade of Nigeria, Ghana, and WAEMU countries. The first four columns of panel A show the pairwise correlations between levels of the terms of trade, while the next four columns show the pairwise correlations between annual changes in the terms of trade. Two different aggregate measures of terms of trade for WAEMU countries have been calculated using arithmetic average or equal weights (WAEMU [1]) and weighted average or different weights based on GDPs of the economies (WAEMU [2]). Panel B shows pairwise correlations of residuals obtained by estimating AR(1) and AR(2) models on the levels of the terms of trade, respectively. These residuals may be viewed as shocks to the terms of trade. The coefficients on the AR(2) term were generally not statistically significant, except for Ghana.

To explore this issue further, panel B of table 4-9 shows the correlations of terms-of-trade shocks hitting these countries. This is based on pairwise correlations of residuals obtained by estimating univariate AR(1) and AR(2) models, respectively, fitted to each country's/region's terms of trade. These residuals may be viewed as shocks to the terms of trade. The coefficients on the AR(2) term were generally not statistically significant, except for Ghana. Hence, we focus more on the results in the first four columns of this panel. The results from this exercise show that shocks to Nigeria's terms of trade are positively correlated with the corresponding measure for Ghana but negatively correlated with that for WAEMU.

Finally, table 4-10 reports results from a principal components analysis on the terms of trade for all of the ECOWAS countries. The first column shows that the first principal component, a measure of the co-movement of the underlying time series, explains about 46 percent of the variance in the levels of the terms of trade. This is a relatively high degree of co-movement, but turns out to be driven largely by co-movement of the terms of trade among WAEMU countries. This can be seen from the results in the second panel, which are based on just WAEMU countries and show that the first principal component explains nearly 60 percent of the variance of the terms of trade in these countries.

Going back to the first panel, the second principal component also turns out to have a large variance contribution, which suggests that there is at least one more group of countries that have somewhat positively correlated terms of trade among themselves but uncorrelated with the first group. The variance contributions of the first principal component drop significantly when considering changes in or shocks to the terms of trade.

In short, there is a limited commonality of terms of trade fluctuations—measured as levels, changes, or shocks—among ECOWAS countries, with a particular lack of symmetry when considering Nigeria and WAEMU.

FINANCIAL INTEGRATION

As discussed in an earlier chapter, the level of trade integration among ECOWAS countries appears relatively limited. Capital mobility is another important criterion for an optimum currency area. However, it is not straightforward to measure the extent of financial integration across coun-

TABLE 4-10. **Principal Components Analysis: Terms of Trade in the ECOWAS Countries**

	ECOWAS			WAEMU		
	(1) Levels	(2) Changes	(3) Residuals	(1) Levels	(2) Changes	(3) Residuals
PC1	0.46	0.22	0.27	0.59	0.33	0.41
PC2	0.28	0.21	0.22	0.20	0.25	0.24

Notes: The left panel shows the proportion of the variances of the levels, changes, and residuals of the annual terms of trade, respectively, accounted for by the first and second principal components for each of these measures for ECOWAS countries except for Niger. The right panel shows the proportion of the variance explained by the two most important principal components (PC1 and PC2) among WAEMU countries. Terms of trade residuals are obtained from univariate AR(1) model estimated on levels of each country's terms of trade. These residuals may be viewed as shocks to the terms of trade.

tries. For example, two countries that have de jure open capital accounts with no restrictions on capital flows across their borders might, in fact, have little actual cross-border capital flows, implying a low level of de facto financial integration. This issue is even more complicated in the context of countries with underdeveloped financial markets.

To examine this issue in the context of ECOWAS countries, we used data from the IMF's Coordinated Direct Investment Survey (CDIS) to examine how much of the stock of inward FDI of countries for which data were available was accounted for by other ECOWAS countries.[9] The second column of table 4-11 shows that, for Benin, Guinea Bissau, and Togo, about a quarter of the outstanding stock of FDI liabilities in 2015 was accounted for by other ECOWAS countries. For the remaining four countries for which data were available—Cabo Verde, Ghana, Niger, and Nigeria—this share was well below 10 percent. This crude measure suggests a limited amount of financial integration among the ECOWAS countries, although it is worth reemphasizing the tentative nature of this exercise because data are so limited.

The last column of table 4-11 contains data on the share of ECOWAS countries' FDI liabilities stock accounted for by eurozone countries. These shares are quite large for all ECOWAS countries for which data are available, not just the WAEMU countries. For instance, more than half of Ghana's outstanding stock of FDI and 40 percent of that for Nigeria are accounted

TABLE 4-11. **ECOWAS Capital Flow Patterns, 2015 (as shares of total FDI liabilities, in percent)**

Selected ECOWAS countries:	Inward direct investment positions from ECOWAS	Inward direct investment positions from Eurozone
Benin*	26.2	—
Cabo Verde	1.7	42.8
Ghana	4.9	54.9
Guinea-Bissau*	25.6	36.1
Niger*	6.2	44.4
Nigeria	1.8	39.6
Togo*	28.4	5.2

*WAEMU Countries

Data sources: Authors' calculations, based on IMF Coordinated Direct Investment Survey (CDIS) and International Financial Statistics (IFS) data.

Notes: Only the ECOWAS countries with both 2015 International Investment Position (IIP) data and CDIS data available are reported under "Selected ECOWAS countries."

for by inward investment from eurozone countries. This level of FDI dependence of ECOWAS on the eurozone is surprising in view of the relatively modest trade relationship between the two areas.

An ECOWAS currency union, presumably with a currency no longer pegged to the euro, would lack this protective mechanism for dealing with a sudden stop or reversal in capital flows that could put stresses on the balance of payments of countries in the region. The ratio of reserves to external debt, a capital account-based (rather than current account-based) criterion for judging reserve adequacy, suggests some vulnerabilities. For instance, reserves cover only about one-third of total WAEMU external debt, which could make it difficult for these countries to meet debt obligations in the event of negative capital flow shocks, especially in circumstances in which international investors are reluctant to roll over loans. These numbers should be interpreted with caution, since a significant portion of WAEMU external debt is accounted for by official concessional debt, which is unlikely to be prone to a capital flow reversal shock.[10]

The exposure of individual ECOWAS countries to capital flow shocks would be substantially reduced if the region had a reserve pooling arrangement. Ghana and Nigeria together had about US$46 billion in reported international reserves at the end of 2019. This suggests that an ECOWAS currency union would have substantial reserves as a buffer against capital flow shocks. This may not, however, prevent capital market stresses from developing if all ECOWAS countries were to be hit by the same shock or by a simultaneous set of shocks. For instance, a positive shock to advanced economy interest rates that leads to capital outflows from emerging markets and developing economies, coupled with a negative shock to oil prices that puts stress on Nigeria's finances, could result in significant balance of payments stress among ECOWAS members.

LABOR MARKETS

A unified and flexible labor market with relatively unimpeded mobility across countries could provide a useful adjustment mechanism in response to country-specific or industry-specific shocks. Large and persistent disparities in labor market outcomes across countries could create tensions during periods of economic stress. This section provides a simple overview of differences in unemployment, employment rates, and wage levels across ECOWAS countries.

There is a wide range of estimated unemployment rates across these countries (see figure 4-1, top panel). In 2019, unemployment rates ranged from just 0.5 percent in Niger to about 10 percent in Cabo Verde, the Gambia, Nigeria, and Mali.

Unemployment figures sometimes tend to be difficult to compare across countries because of conceptual differences, particularly related to how active labor force participation is defined.[11] The ratio of total employment to the working-age population (that is, the potential labor force) tends to be a more informative measure than the unemployment rate. The lower panel of figure 4-1 shows that the employment ratio in 2019 ranges between 70 and 80 percent in Guinea-Bissau, Liberia, Niger, and Togo to below 50 percent in Nigeria and Senegal.

The bottom line is that there are substantial differences in labor market outcomes across ECOWAS countries. These differences, in tandem with differences in average wages and broader living standards (as measured, for instance, by per capita incomes), could create some short-term social and political tensions within the region as it attempts to implement a common monetary framework. Such tensions would intensify if the movement of labor across countries—which, in principle, is now relatively free across ECOWAS—becomes a key source of cross-country adjustment in the absence of further convergence of macroeconomic and labor market indicators.

PRODUCTIVITY AND COMPETITIVENESS

One of the key challenges to the stability of a currency union comes from differential levels of productivity and, hence, external competitiveness within the union. Such differentials can generate centrifugal forces if the cyclical positions of different countries within the zone require different policy responses, but monetary policy is determined at a central level by zone-wide considerations. With fiscal policy constrained as well, this would require significant internal adjustment in the form of wage adjustment in order for a country to maintain its external competitiveness.

In order to evaluate the economic tensions that could be precipitated by such an adjustment, it is useful to begin by evaluating initial conditions—levels of productivity and competitiveness across members of the proposed zone.[12] There are substantial cross-country differences in labor productivity in agriculture, with Nigeria registering productivity in this sector that

FIGURE 4-1. **Unemployment and Employment Rates in ECOWAS (2019)**

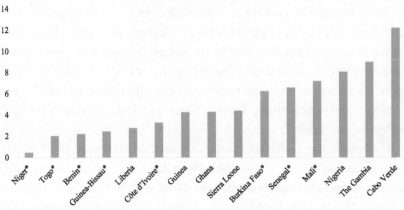

Unemployment Rate (in percent)

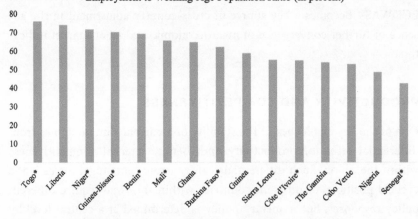

Employment to Working-Age Population Ratio (in percent)

Data sources: International Labor Organization, ILO modeled estimates.

Notes: The top panel shows the ILO-modeled unemployment rate in each country. The employment ratios in the lower panel represent the ratios of total employment to the total working-age (15–64) population in each country. The asterisks denote WAEMU countries.

is more than four times that in eleven other countries. The relative cross-country differentials in industry are smaller than in agriculture, but still quite large. Labor productivity in industry is at least three times higher in Nigeria than in eight other countries. Comparing the two largest economies, labor productivity in Nigeria is at least double that in Ghana.

A different measure of a country's overall competitiveness comes from the World Economic Forum's (WEF) Global Competitiveness Index.[13] According to the WEF, this index "assesses the factors and institutions identified by empirical and theoretical research as determining improvements in productivity, which, in turn, is the main determinant of long-term growth and an essential factor in economic growth and prosperity." All ECOWAS countries for which data on this index are available fare poorly in an international comparison. The 2017 rankings of the countries range from 106th in the world for Senegal to 134th in the world for Liberia. Ghana and Nigeria come in at 111th and 125th in the world, respectively. For these two countries, their rankings in 2017 represent a ten-point deterioration relative to their rankings in 2012. The countries that improved their rankings over this period are Senegal, Cabo Verde, Guinea, Mali, and Sierra Leone.

The implications are that ECOWAS countries face significant challenges, both in terms of their low levels of international competitiveness and the divergence of productivity levels across the members of the proposed single currency zone. It will, therefore, be important to carefully evaluate the flexibility of internal adjustment mechanisms, especially those related to the labor and product markets, in responding to common, as well as country-specific, shocks.

5

Exchange Rate and Monetary Policy Regimes

This chapter provides a descriptive overview of the monetary and exchange rate regimes prevalent among ECOWAS countries and a comparison with those of other emerging and developing economies around the world. Since the degree of capital account openness has implications for evaluating optimal regimes, this is discussed as well.

This chapter is based on the 2017 IMF Annual Report on Exchange Arrangements and Exchange Restrictions (AREAER). The AREAER provides information about de facto exchange rate management practices. In some cases, these are distinct from de jure exchange rate regimes. This distinction is an important one for the purposes of this study—how central banks actually manage exchange rates, as opposed to their stated policies, is an important distinction when considering a transition to a new regime. This is particularly relevant for emerging market economies, since their exchange rate policies can affect monetary policy implementation. A country that has a de facto tightly managed exchange rate will tend to have less monetary policy autonomy, unless it has very tight and nonporous capital controls.

ECOWAS COUNTRIES

Table 5-1 provides a listing of exchange rate and monetary policy regimes in ECOWAS countries. The eight WAEMU countries, of course, maintain an exchange rate pegged to the euro, which implies that they have no independent monetary policy. Liberia has an exchange rate that is managed relative to the U.S. dollar, thereby ceding some of its monetary independence. The Gambia, Guinea, and Sierra Leone actively manage their exchange rates, and their monetary policy is anchored through targeting of monetary aggregates.

That leaves the two largest economies in ECOWAS, which have starkly different regimes. Nigeria targets a monetary aggregate but also maintains a de facto exchange rate anchor relative to the U.S. dollar. In addition, Nigeria has multiple exchange rates, an official one as well as a market exchange rate that is tolerated by the authorities (it is not an unauthorized black-market rate).[1] Ghana, by contrast, has a floating exchange rate and an explicit inflation target that provides a nominal anchor.

As this discussion suggests, there is a wide disparity of exchange rate and monetary regimes among the ECOWAS countries. This will pose some challenges, both during the transition and in the process of administering a currency union.

One consideration that is relevant for these transitional issues, as well as for thinking about the end point, is the degree of capital account openness of these countries. Table 5-2, drawn from country reports in the AREAER, shows whether or not ECOWAS countries have restrictions on different categories of capital flows. The WAEMU countries, along with Guinea and Sierra Leone, have a broad array of capital controls. Out of eleven categories of capital account transactions, these countries have restrictions in ten categories. These countries also have some restrictions on current account transactions; in particular, they have repatriation requirements on proceeds from exports and invisible transactions. At the other extreme are the Gambia and Liberia, which have relatively open capital accounts, including on financial flows related to current account transactions.

Nigeria has not yet acceded to Article VIII of the IMF Articles of Agreement. It is one of the few member countries of the IMF that has not yet done so.[2] The IMF summarizes the obligations under this article as follows: "Under Article VIII, Sections 2, 3, and 4, IMF members undertake not to impose restrictions on the making of payments and transfers for current

TABLE 5-1. Exchange Rate Regimes and Monetary Policy Frameworks (ECOWAS, 2017)

Exchange Rate Arrangement (No. of countries: 192)	Exchange Rate Peg				Monetary aggregate target (24)	Inflation-targeting (40)	Other (46)
	U.S. dollar (39)	Euro (25)	Composite (9)	Other (9)			
Conventional peg (43)		Cabo Verde, WAEMU (Benin, Burkina Faso, Côte d'Ivoire, Guinea Bissau, Mali, Niger, Senegal and Togo)					
Stabilized arrangement (24)					Nigeria*		
Other managed arrangement (18)	Liberia				The Gambia, Guinea and Sierra Leone		
Floating (38)						Ghana	

Data source: IMF Annual Report on Exchange Arrangements and Exchange Restrictions, 2017.

*Nigeria maintains a de facto exchange rate anchor to the U.S. dollar.

TABLE 5-2. Exchange Rate Regimes and Liberalization of Capital Movements (ECOWAS, 2017)

	Fixed Exchange Rate Regime		Managed Exchange Rate Regime			Flexible Exchange Rate Regime		
	WAEMU	Cabo Verde	The Gambia	Liberia	Nigeria	Ghana	Guinea	Sierra Leone
Currency	CFA franc	Escudo	Dalasi	USD and Liberian US$	Naira	Cedi	Guinean franc	Leone
Accession to Articles VIII of the IMF statutes	Yes	Yes	Yes	No	No	Yes	Yes	Yes
Controls on payments for invisible transactions and current transfers	Yes	Yes	No	No	Yes	Yes	Yes	Yes
Proceeds from exports and/or invisible transactions								
Repatriation requirements	Yes	Yes	No	No	Yes	Yes	Yes	Yes
Surrender requirements	Yes	Yes	No	Yes	Yes	Yes	No	No
Capital transactions								
On capital market securities	Yes	No	No	No	Yes	Yes	Yes	Yes
On money market instruments	Yes	Yes	No	No	Yes	Yes	Yes	Yes
On collective investment securities	Yes	No	No	No	No	Yes	Yes	Yes
Controls on derivatives and other instruments	Yes	N/A	No	No	No	No	Yes	Yes
Commercial credits	Yes	Yes	No	No	Yes	No	Yes	Yes
Financial credits	Yes	Yes	Yes	No	No	No	Yes	Yes
Guarantees, securities, and financial backup facilities	Yes	Yes	No	No	No	Yes	Yes	Yes
Controls on direct investment	Yes	Yes	No	No	No	No	Yes	Yes
Controls on liquidation of direct investment	No	No	No	No	No	Yes	No	Yes
Controls on real estate transactions	Yes	Yes	No	No	No	No	Yes	Yes
Controls on personal capital transactions	Yes	Yes	No	No	Yes	Yes	Yes	Yes
Provisions specific to:								
Commercial banks and other credit institutions	Yes	Yes	Yes	Yes	Yes	Yes	Yes	Yes
Institutional investors	Yes	N/A	Yes	Yes	Yes	Yes	N/A	Yes

Data source: IMF Annual Report on Exchange Arrangements and Exchange Restrictions, 2017.

Notes: "Yes" indicates that there are restrictions on capital flows in the relevant category.

international transactions, and not to engage in, or permit any of their fiscal agencies to engage in, any discriminatory currency arrangement or multiple currency practice, except with IMF approval." Such restrictions on financial flows, along with Nigeria's multiple exchange rates and de facto anchoring of the naira relative to the U.S. dollar, complicate any discussions of a move toward an ECOWAS currency union.

The other major economy, Ghana, has acceded to Article VIII, but, according to the IMF, still maintains various restrictions on financial flows related to current account transactions. Ghana has an open capital account in certain key categories, including personal capital transactions, but, overall, still has a relatively closed capital account, with restrictions in six of eleven capital account transaction categories.

The main takeaway from this discussion is that there are substantial differences across ECOWAS countries in terms of their exchange rate and monetary arrangements. Moreover, the disparities in capital account openness could complicate the management of whatever exchange rate regime is chosen for the eventual currency union.

A CONCEPTUAL REVIEW

There has been a long and vigorous debate about whether there are economic forces that inexorably drive countries, especially developing ones, toward one of two extreme exchange rate regimes, either hard pegs or free floats. This bipolar view was refuted by Fischer (2001), who argued that for countries open to international capital flows, softly pegged exchange rates are crisis-prone and not sustainable over long periods. He noted that a wide variety of flexible rate arrangements remains possible for such countries.

The recent academic literature has tended to the view that a flexible exchange rate regime, along with a nominal anchor provided by an inflation targeting regime, is the best option for a small open economy, or even a large and open emerging market economy.[3] This combination is seen as providing monetary stability in the form of low inflation, while the flexible exchange rate provides a buffer against external shocks. An increasing number of emerging market economies have adopted this combination, although giving themselves room to smooth out short-term exchange rate fluctuations. The Reserve Bank of India, for instance, follows this policy of "leaning against the wind," which entails limiting short-term exchange rate volatility while not fundamentally resisting, through foreign exchange market intervention, market pressures pushing the currency in one direction or the other.

The choice of exchange rate regimes is, of course, determined to a large extent by factors such as economic size, degree of trade and financial openness, economic structure, and nature of shocks that an economy is subject to. The evolving consensus in the academic literature is that a flexible exchange rate, and the monetary policy autonomy that comes with it, can provide a useful shock absorption mechanism for emerging markets and developing economies that are exposed to a wide array of external shocks.

There are two important qualifications to this proposition, however. The first is that a combination of a more flexible exchange rate and open capital account can make a developing economy more vulnerable to global financial cycles, including monetary policy spillovers from advanced economies that can trigger capital flow volatility.

The second is that the degree of shock absorption is affected by the currency denomination of a country's foreign trade. In particular, the paradigm of dominant currency pricing has important implications for this issue.[4] If a country's external trade is largely denominated in a major international currency such as the U.S. dollar, rather than in the currencies of the home country or its trading partners, a flexible exchange rate regime might yield much weaker shock absorption.

The latter point is an important twist to the notion that exchange rate flexibility provides an absorption mechanism against external shocks. Such flexibility is based on the notion that, for instance, in the face of weak external demand or negative terms-of-trade shock, a currency depreciation would boost external competitiveness, increase exports, and help offset some of the falls in domestic economic activity. An exchange rate depreciation could, of course, stoke domestic inflation, which is why the associated inflation-targeting policy becomes important in order to ensure price stability over the medium to long term.

However, this logic depends on the currency of invoicing of a country's external trade, especially its exports. Recent literature shows that the implications can be very different, depending on whether a country's external trade follows local currency pricing (LCP), producer currency pricing (PCP), or dominant currency pricing (DCP). The DCP model is one in which a country's external trade is largely denominated in a dominant currency such as the U.S. dollar, even if the home country's trade is mostly with countries other than the United States. This, in tandem with certain other conditions (pricing complementarities and imported input use in production) can offset some of the stabilizing effects of a flexible exchange rate.

Initial conditions also matter. A country with a large volume of foreign currency–denominated external debt, issued either by the sovereign or the corporate sector, could face significant budgetary and corporate balance sheet pressures if it switched from a managed to a floating exchange rate and found its currency depreciating. In such circumstances, a flexible exchange rate could exacerbate rather than dampen external shocks. Moreover, fiscal dominance can also threaten price stability in the absence of a nominal anchor such as a fixed exchange rate.

PRACTICES IN OTHER DEVELOPING AND EMERGING MARKET ECONOMIES

One striking development over the last two decades has been the shift away from pegged or tightly managed exchange rate regimes. The Asian financial crisis of 1997–98, along with many other country-specific balance-of-payments crises, led to a reconsideration of the benefit-risk tradeoffs of pegged exchange rates. The new favored paradigm—inflation targeting and flexible exchange rates—began to take hold in the 2000s and has continued to perpetuate, despite some questions arising about the viability of this framework during the global financial crisis.

Before gauging practices in other countries, it is worth categorizing the wide possible array of exchange rate and monetary policy arrangements. Reinhart and Rogoff (2004) provide a granular decomposition of different types of exchange rate regimes, indicating the importance of even seemingly modest and subtle differences—especially in terms of the way they are practiced—across some similar-looking regimes. The IMF provides a more tractable categorization, which is reproduced in table 5-3. Figure 5-1 provides a categorical overview of key alternatives. Some countries simply abandon any pretense of domestic monetary policy and use a foreign currency—full dollarization. Among countries that do have their own currencies, currency boards and conventional pegs constitute one extreme while floating exchange rates constitute the other. There is a large set of intermediate regimes that are practiced by various countries.

Table 5-4 lists a few broad categories of monetary policy frameworks. In the case of fixed exchange rates, it is the exchange rate itself that provides the nominal anchor for monetary policy. For other countries, the main

TABLE 5-3. IMF Exchange Rate Arrangements Descriptions

No separate legal tender	The currency of another country circulates as the sole legal tender (formal dollarization). Adopting such an arrangement implies the complete surrender by the monetary authorities of control over domestic monetary policy.
Currency board	A currency board arrangement is a monetary arrangement based on an explicit legislative commitment to exchange domestic currency for a specified foreign currency at a fixed exchange rate, combined with restrictions on the issuing authority to ensure the fulfillment of its legal obligation.
Conventional peg	For this category, the country formally (de jure) pegs its currency at a fixed rate to another currency or basket of currencies, where the basket is formed, for example, from the currencies of major trading or financial partners and weights reflect the geographic distribution of trade, services, or capital flows.
Stabilized arrangement	Classification as a stabilized arrangement entails a spot market exchange rate that remains within a margin of 2 percent for six months or more (with the exception of a specified number of outliers or step adjustments) and is not floating.
Crawling peg	The currency is adjusted in small amounts at a fixed rate or in response to changes in selected quantitative indicators, such as past inflation differentials vis-à-vis major trading partners or differentials between the inflation target and expected inflation in major trading partners.
Crawl-like arrangement	For classification as a crawl-like arrangement, the exchange rate must remain within a narrow margin of 2 percent relative to a statistically identified trend for six months or more (with the exception of a specified number of outliers) and the exchange rate arrangement cannot be considered as floating.
Pegged exchange rate within horizontal bands	The value of the currency is maintained within certain margins of fluctuation of at least ±1 percent around a fixed central rate, or the margin between the maximum and minimum value of the exchange rate exceeds 2 percent.
Other managed arrangement	This category is a residual and is used when the exchange rate arrangement does not meet the criteria for any of the other categories. Arrangements characterized by frequent shifts in policies may fall into this category.
Floating	A floating exchange rate is largely market-determined, without an ascertainable or predictable path for the rate.
Free floating	A floating exchange rate can be classified as free floating if intervention occurs only exceptionally and aims to address disorderly market conditions and if the authorities have provided information or data confirming that intervention has been limited to at most three instances in the previous six months, each lasting no more than three business days.

Source: IMF AREAER Compilation Guide, 2017.

FIGURE 5-1. Exchange Rate Regime Classification

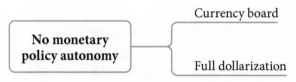

No monetary policy autonomy
- Currency board
- Full dollarization

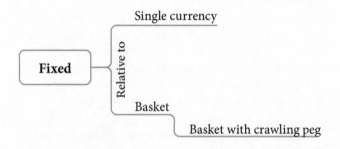

Fixed — Relative to
- Single currency
- Basket
- Basket with crawling peg

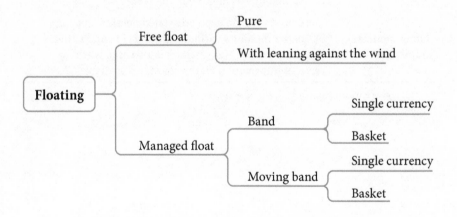

Floating
- Free float
  - Pure
  - With leaning against the wind
- Managed float
  - Band
    - Single currency
    - Basket
  - Moving band
    - Single currency
    - Basket

TABLE 5-4. IMF Monetary Policy Framework Descriptions

Exchange rate peg	The monetary authority buys or sells foreign exchange to maintain the exchange rate at its predetermined level or within a range. The exchange rate thus serves as the nominal anchor or intermediate target of monetary policy.
Monetary aggregate target	The intermediate target of monetary policy is a monetary aggregate such as M0, M1, or M2, although the country may also set targets for inflation. The central bank may use a quantity (central bank reserves or base money) or price variable (policy rate) as operational target.
Inflation-targeting framework	This involves the public announcement of numerical targets for inflation, with an institutional commitment by the monetary authority to achieve these targets, typically over a medium-term horizon.
Other monetary framework	The country has no explicitly stated nominal anchor, but rather monitors various indicators in conducting monetary policy. This category is also used when no relevant information on the country is available.

Source: IMF AREAER Compilation Guide, 2017.

types of frameworks include those that target a monetary aggregate, those that target inflation, and those that do not have an explicit nominal anchor but use a variety of indicators to conduct monetary policy.

Table 5-5 shows where the emerging markets fall in this spectrum of possibilities. The twenty-five countries included in the table are those in the MSCI Emerging Markets Index (except Taiwan) and also include Argentina and Saudi Arabia. A majority of emerging market economies now pursue inflation targeting regimes, with sixteen of those having floating or freely floating exchange rates. This includes a number of countries—such as Brazil, Chile, and Russia—that are classified as commodity exporters. It is interesting to note that three oil exporters in the sample—Qatar, Saudi Arabia, and the UAE—peg their currencies to the U.S. dollar. Virtually all oil contracts continue to be denominated in U.S. dollars, which is the historical justification for this arrangement. However, with even countries such as Saudi Arabia attempting to diversify their economies, the suitability of the dollar peg has been a subject of considerable policy debate.

China is the lone emerging market that, until recently, used a monetary aggregate target as an anchor for monetary policy. The People's Bank of China (PBOC) now targets the seven-day repurchase rate for depository institutions as its key policy rate, rather than specifying credit growth targets. The interest rate is managed within a corridor. The floor is the rate paid on commercial banks' excess reserves held at the PBOC. The ceiling is the rate at which banks can borrow from the PBOC through the standing lending facility. The PBOC uses open market operations, including regular injections and withdrawals of liquidity, to keep its policy rate close to the middle of this corridor.[5]

The table also shows (in parentheses in each row and column) the full set of IMF member countries that have adopted each exchange rate and monetary policy regimes. Sixty-nine of the 192 countries have floating or freely floating exchange rates, sixty-seven have a peg of one form or another (including those with no legal tender of their own, and those with a currency board or conventional peg). This would seem to suggest some support for the bipolarity hypothesis, although that leaves fifty-six countries with managed but not pegged exchange rates.

In terms of monetary policy frameworks, sixty-four have currencies that are pegged to the U.S. dollar or euro. Among the countries that do have independent monetary policy, forty have inflation targeting regimes, which is more than any other single regime (the category "Other" includes a variety

TABLE 5-5. **Exchange Rate Regime and Monetary Policy Frameworks (Emerging Market Economies, 2017)**

Exchange rate arrangement (no. of countries: 192)	Exchange rate peg				Monetary aggregate target (24)	Inflation-targeting (40)	Other (46)
	U.S. dollar (39)	Euro (25)	Composite (9)	Other (9)			
No separate legal tender (13)							
Currency board (11)							
Conventional peg (43)	Qatar,* Saudi Arabia,* UAE*						
Stabilized arrangement (24)					China	Czech Republic	Pakistan
Crawling peg (3)							
Crawl-like arrangement (10)							
Pegged exchange rate within horizontal bands (1)							
Other managed arrangement (18)							
Floating (38)						Argentina,* Brazil,* Colombia,* Hungary, India, Indonesia,* Korea, Peru,* Philippines, South Africa,* Thailand, Turkey	Egypt, Malaysia*
Free floating (31)						Chile,* Mexico, Poland, Russia*	Greece

Source: IMF Annual Report on Exchange Arrangements and Exchange Restrictions, 2017

Notes: The above table includes Argentina, Saudi Arabia, and countries listed in the MSCI Emerging Markets Index (except Taiwan). China maintains a de facto exchange rate anchor to a composite currency basket. Czech Republic maintains a de facto exchange rate anchor to the euro. Pakistan maintains a de facto exchange rate anchor to the U.S. dollar. Greece is a member of the Eurozone but is now classified as an emerging economy. A country marked with an asterisk is classified as a commodity exporter by the World Bank. An economy is defined as a commodity exporter when, on average in 2012–2014, either (1) total commodities exports accounted for 30 percent or more of total goods exports or (2) exports of any single commodity accounted for 20 percent or more of total goods exports. This taxonomy results in some well-diversified economies not being classified under this category, even if they are exporters of certain commodities (for example, Mexico).

of monetary arrangements). In short, there is no clear consensus—at least in terms of observed practices—about what exchange rate and monetary policy frameworks are optimal, with the answer depending, to a large extent, on the specific economic and structural characteristics of each country.

Later in this book, in chapter 7, we will examine the different monetary and exchange rate arrangements among the ECOWAS countries, and potential challenges they face in converging on a single framework. Before discussing those challenges, in chapter 6, we turn to an exploration of how such a framework might actually work, by conducting some illustrative experiments based on simple Taylor rules and examining their implications for policy settings within an ECOWAS currency union.

6

Illustrative Monetary Policy Rules

This chapter presents some analysis to show how monetary policy rules might operate within ECOWAS.[1] The analysis aims at a characterization of what sorts of rules central banks in the region follow in practice, along with some perspectives on how such rules might have worked if ECOWAS, in fact, had a common monetary policy.

The Taylor rule provides a useful characterization of monetary policy formulation in advanced economies. Its relevance for developing economies—which face additional issues such as fiscal dominance, capital flow volatility, underdeveloped financial markets, weak and uncertain monetary transmission mechanisms, and a desire for exchange rate stability—is less obvious.[2] However, variants of the Taylor rule provide a useful benchmark for thinking about how inflation targeting might work within an ECOWAS currency union.

KEY MACROECONOMIC VARIABLES

Before proceeding with the analysis of monetary policy rules, we examine the behavior of key macroeconomic aggregates in ECOWAS countries. From the perspective of a proposed currency union, as noted earlier, the comovement of GDP is an important criterion. Figure 6-1 shows annual GDP growth over the period 2009–17 for Nigeria, along with composite measures of growth for the remaining ECOWAS countries and for just the WAEMU countries. The correlation between GDP growth in Nigeria and in the rest of ECOWAS over this period is –0.31, while the corresponding correlation with WAEMU growth is –0.49.[3]

Figure 6-2 examines the relationship between CPI inflation in Nigeria and the rest of ECOWAS. The levels of inflation are consistently higher in Nigeria than in the rest of ECOWAS and substantially higher than in the WAEMU countries. The correlation between CPI inflation in Nigeria and that in the rest of ECOWAS is –0.05 over the full sample and –0.11 over the period 2009–15. The corresponding correlations with WAEMU inflation are –0.09 and 0.37, respectively.

A different measure of inflation, based on the GDP deflator, is shown in figure 6-3. By this measure, inflation in Nigeria is more in line with inflation in the rest of ECOWAS, although still significantly higher for most of 2010–17 relative to WAEMU inflation. The correlation of this measure of inflation between Nigeria and the rest of ECOWAS is relatively high (0.46 for 2009–17); the same is true for the correlation with inflation in WAEMU (0.33 for 2009–17).

Taken together, these results point to some challenges in managing monetary policy for an ECOWAS currency union where there are significant divergences in output growth and inflation.

In order to provide a rough evaluation of relative monetary policy stances in the ECOWAS region, figure 6-4 plots various measures of nominal interest rates. Panel A shows that the policy rate in both Nigeria and Ghana, the two largest economies, has been substantially higher than in WAEMU over the period 2009–17. Nominal deposit rates in Nigeria have been more in line with those of other ECOWAS countries and the WAEMU, although the level of volatility in Nigeria's deposit rates is much greater than is the case for other country groups.

Figure 6-5 plots CPI inflation-adjusted real interest rates that correspond to the nominal rates shown in figure 6-4. The real policy rate in Nigeria has

FIGURE 6-1. **Annual GDP Growth**
(in percent)

A. Market exchange rates

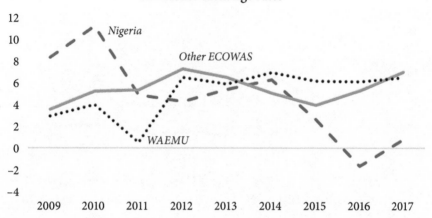

B. PPP exchange rates

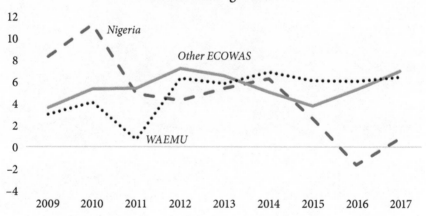

Data source: The World Bank.

Notes: The growth rates in panel A are based on GDP converted to constant 2010 U.S. dollars using 2010 market exchange rates, while those in panel B are based on GDP converted to constant 2011 international dollars using purchasing power parity exchange rates. "Other ECOWAS" comprises the other fourteen ECOWAS countries, excluding Nigeria. Average growth rates for country groups are weighted by country GDP.

FIGURE 6-2. **CPI Inflation**
(in percent)

A. Nominal GDP weights, market exchange rates

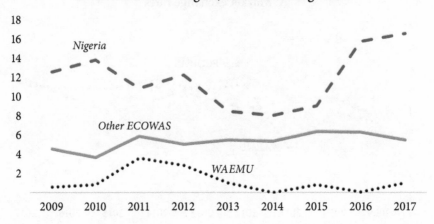

B. Nominal GDP weights, PPP exchange rates

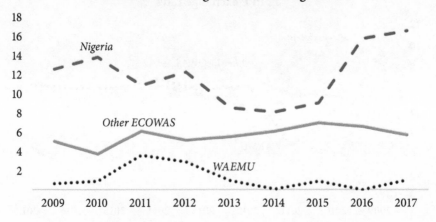

Data sources: The World Bank and IMF

Notes: The inflation rates in both panels are based on annual growth rates of the CPI index. Average inflation rates for country groups are weighted by GDP converted to current U.S. dollars using average market exchange rates in panel A, and are weighted by GDP converted to current U.S. dollars using purchasing power parity exchange rates in panel B.

FIGURE 6-3. Inflation Based on GDP Deflator
(in percent)

A. Nominal GDP weights, market exchange rates

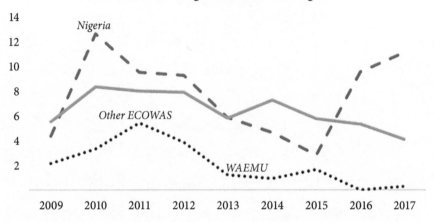

B. Nominal GDP weights, PPP exchange rates

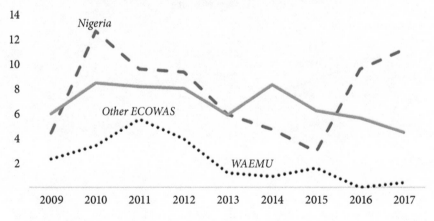

Data sources: The World Bank and IMF.

Notes: The inflation rates in both panels are based on annual growth rates of the GDP deflator. Average inflation rates for country groups are weighted by GDP converted to current U.S. dollars using average market exchange rates in panel A, and are weighted by GDP converted to current U.S. dollars using purchasing power parity exchange rates in panel B.

FIGURE 6-4. **Nominal Interest Rates**

(in percent)

A. Policy rate

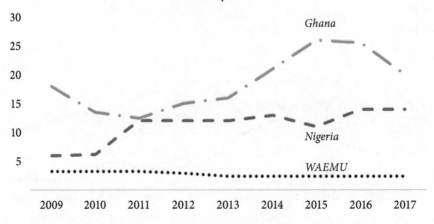

B. Deposit rate

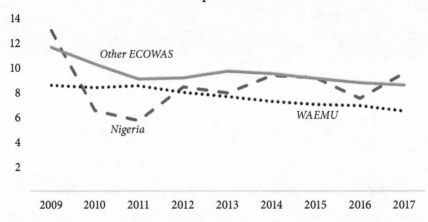

Data sources: The World Bank and IMF.

Notes: Panel A shows policy interest rates and panel B shows deposit rates. Interest rates for country groups are weighted by GDP converted to 2011 international dollars using purchasing power parity rates. "Other ECOWAS" comprises the other fourteen ECOWAS countries, excluding Nigeria. Panel A compares Nigeria and Ghana with WAEMU countries because data for other countries are unavailable.

tended to differ quite significantly from that in Ghana and the WAEMU. In 2009–10 and 2016–17, the real policy rate in Nigeria was, in fact, negative while it was positive in Ghana and WAEMU. It is interesting to note that the real policy rate for Ghana has been substantially higher than that of either Nigeria or WAEMU for much of the last decade. Real deposit rates in Nigeria have typically been much lower than those in the rest of ECOWAS or WAEMU, with high inflation often pushing Nigeria's real deposit rate into substantially negative territory over most of the last decade.

The picture presented by these data is one of the significant challenges that could be posed by differences in economic conjunctures of Nigeria and other ECOWAS countries and also by the differences in associated monetary policy stances.

TAYLOR RULE ESTIMATES FOR NIGERIA, GHANA, WAEMU

First, we estimate simple Taylor rules for Nigeria, Ghana, and WAEMU using annual data over the period 2001–18. Other ECOWAS economies were excluded due to data constraints. The estimated regressions encompass various combinations of the deviation of inflation from its target, the output gap, and the lagged policy rate:

(1)   Policy rate = inflation deviation from target
            + output gap + lagged policy rate

$$i_t = \delta_0 + \delta_1 \cdot (\pi_t - \pi_{Target}) + \delta_2 \cdot y_t + \lambda \cdot i_{t-1} + \varepsilon_t$$

(2)   Policy rate = inflation deviation from target + lagged policy rate

$$i_t = \delta_0 + \delta_1 \cdot (\pi_t - \pi_{Target}) + \lambda \cdot i_{t-1} + \varepsilon_t$$

(3)   Policy rate = inflation deviation from target

$$i_t = \delta_0 + \delta_1 \cdot (\pi_t - \pi_{Target}) + \varepsilon_t$$

(4)   Policy rate = output gap + lagged policy rate

$$i_t = \delta_0 + \delta_1 \cdot y_t + \lambda \cdot i_{t-1} + \varepsilon_t$$

(5)   Policy rate = inflation deviation + output gap

$$i_t = \delta_0 + \delta_1 \cdot (\pi_t - \pi_{Target}) + \delta_2 \cdot y_t + \varepsilon_t$$

Drawing on proposals under consideration by ECOWAS leaders, the inflation target is set at 6 percent.[4] The output gap, defined as the difference between actual and potential (or trend) output, is calculated by detrend-

FIGURE 6-5. **Real Interest Rates**

(in percent)

A. Policy rate

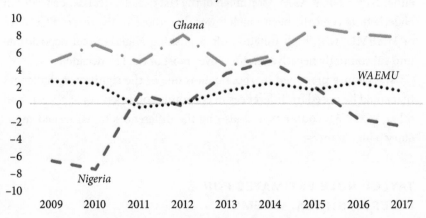

B. Deposit rate

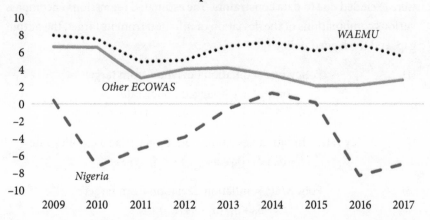

Data sources: The World Bank and IMF.

Notes: Panel A shows policy interest rates and panel B shows deposit rates. Interest rates for country groups are weighted by GDP. "Other ECOWAS" comprises the other fourteen ECOWAS countries, excluding Nigeria. Panel A compares Nigeria and Ghana with WAEMU countries because data for other countries are unavailable.

ing log GDP using either the Hodrick-Prescott filter or a linear time trend. The specification includes a lagged interest rate term to take account of the well established result that, in both advanced and developing economies, the policy interest rate tends to be highly persistent.[5] Appendix D has a full list of variables used in the analysis and descriptions of how they are constructed.

The results of estimating these regressions for Nigeria are shown in table 6-1. The coefficient on the lagged policy rate is significant in all specifications in which it appears, consistent with the results in the literature for most advanced and developing economies. The coefficient on CPI inflation is positive in specifications (2) and (3) that do not include measures of the output gap. However, the coefficient loses significance in all specifications that include the output gap. The coefficient on the output gap, whether constructed relative to a linear trend or HP-filtered measure of potential output, is negative. This is, of course, contrary to the standard presumption that a positive output gap (output higher than trend) will lead to inflationary pressures and therefore require monetary tightening. In Nigeria's case, the likely reason for this result is that the output gap is driven by terms of trade fluctuations—specifically, oil prices—so that a positive gap is not associated with domestic inflationary pressures.

The next set of regressions explicitly include exchange rates in the Taylor rule calculations. For many developing economies, nominal exchange rate stability—usually expressed relative to the U.S. dollar or another major currency—is an objective of monetary policy. From an econometric perspective, the right variable to include in the regressions is the change in the exchange rate, since this variable tends to be nonstationary in levels. However, we also estimate a specification including the level of the exchange rate, since much of the emphasis in policymaking (and related market commentary) tends to be about the stability of the level of the exchange rate. In these regressions, which are specified below, we use only the HP-filtered output gap:

(6) Policy rate = inflation deviation + output gap + XR + lagged policy rate

$$i_t = \delta_0 + \delta_1 \cdot (\pi_t - \pi_{Target}) + \delta_2 \cdot y_t + \delta_3 \cdot XR_t + \lambda \cdot i_{t-1} + \varepsilon_t$$

(7)   Policy rate = inflation deviation + output gap + XR

$$i_t = \delta_0 + \delta_1 \cdot (\pi_t - \pi_{Target}) + \delta_2 \cdot y_t + \delta_3 \cdot XR_t + \varepsilon_t$$

(8)   Policy rate = inflation deviation + XR + lagged policy rate

$$i_t = \delta_0 + \delta_1 \cdot (\pi_t - \pi_{Target}) + \delta_2 \cdot XR_t + \lambda \cdot i_{t-1} + \varepsilon_t$$

TABLE 6-1. Taylor Rule Estimates (Nigeria)

Model	(1.1) CPI + Output + Lag	(1.2) CPI + Output + Lag	(2) CPI + Lag	(3) CPI Only	(4.1) Output + Lag	(4.2) Output + Lag	(5.1) CPI + Output	(5.2) CPI + Output
CPI	0.223 (0.180)	0.215 (0.176)	0.318* (0.172)	0.392* (0.198)			0.299 (0.180)	0.242 (0.168)
Output_Gap_HP	-0.257 (0.182)				-0.342* (0.172)		-0.397** (0.168)	
Output_Gap_Linear		-0.152 (0.097)				-0.196** (0.091)		-0.252*** (0.081)
Policy_Rate_Lag	0.510** (0.181)	0.433** (0.195)	0.578*** (0.180)		0.544*** (0.182)	0.447** (0.197)		
Constant	4.805* (2.467)	5.763* (2.700)	3.209 (2.264)	10.11*** (1.411)	5.840** (2.363)	6.986** (2.547)	10.72*** (1.279)	11.02*** (1.184)
Observations	18	18	18	19	18	18	19	19
R-squared	0.610	0.622	0.555	0.187	0.568	0.582	0.396	0.494

Notes: Standard errors are reported in parentheses below coefficient estimates. Asterisks indicate statistical significance at the 1 percent (***), 5 percent (**), and 10 percent (*) levels, respectively.

(9) $$\text{Policy rate} = \text{output gap} + \text{XR}$$
$$i_t = \delta_0 + \delta_1 \cdot y_t + \delta_2 \cdot XR_t + \varepsilon_t$$

Table 6-2 shows the results of these extended regressions for Nigeria. The results shown in the previous table remain largely unaffected, with neither the level nor the change in the exchange rate entering with a statistically significant coefficient in any of the regressions.

Tables 6-3 and 6-4 show the corresponding results for Ghana. In table 6-3, the coefficient on CPI inflation is consistently positive, large, and statistically significant. This reflects the inflation targeting framework of the Bank of Ghana, which emphasizes price stability. The coefficient estimates from specifications (1.1) and (1.2), which include the output gap as well as the lagged policy rate, suggest that a 1 percentage point increase in CPI inflation is associated with about a 0.25 percentage point (contemporaneous) increase in the policy rate. These models fit the data for Ghana better than they do for Nigeria, with higher Rsquareds.

Note that in table 6-4, the coefficient on inflation becomes smaller and loses statistical significance in specifications (6.2) and (8.2), which include changes in the nominal exchange rate. Thus, it appears that the Bank of Ghana's policy rates are significantly affected by exchange rate changes, presumably because of their pass-through effects on domestic inflation. The correlation between exchange rate changes and inflation presumably drives this result, which warrants further analysis of such pass-through effects in Ghana as well as other ECOWAS economies.

The results for WAEMU, shown in tables 6-5 and 6-6, are similar to those for Ghana. The coefficients on CPI inflation are generally positive and significant in table 6-5, although they are smaller than in the case of Ghana. The output gap, measured relative to a linear trend, enters with a positive coefficient in specifications (1.2) and (5.2), but the coefficients are small. In table 6-6, the coefficient on inflation remains significant while the coefficients on the level of the exchange rate are consistently positive and significant (specifications (6.1), (7.1), (8.1), and (9.1)). This result reflects the CFA franc peg to the euro, which implies that monetary policy has to emphasize nominal exchange rate stability.

TABLE 6-2. Taylor Rules with Exchange Rates (Estimates for Nigeria)

Model	(6.1)	(6.2)	(7.1)	(7.2)	(8.1)	(8.2)	(9.1)	(9.2)
	CPI + Output + XR + Lag		CPI + Output + XR		CPI + XR + Lag		Output + XR	
CPI	0.217	0.259	0.327*	0.345	0.314	0.349*		
	(0.184)	(0.188)	(0.183)	(0.224)	(0.180)	(0.186)		
Output_Gap_HP	−0.326	−0.282	−0.442**	−0.423*			−0.493**	−0.551**
	(0.215)	(0.187)	(0.176)	(0.217)			(0.185)	(0.210)
Policy_Rate_Lag	0.485**	0.499**			0.579***	0.576***		
	(0.189)	(0.184)			(0.186)	(0.184)		
AVG_FC_USD	−0.007		−0.011		0.001		−0.008	
	(0.012)		(0.012)		(0.011)		(0.013)	
Change_FC		−0.046		−0.057		−0.031		−0.031
		(0.059)		(0.071)		(0.060)		(0.072)
Constant	5.106	3.468	10.37***	8.760***	1.100	1.157	13.79***	12.92***
	(3.997)	(3.050)	(2.761)	(2.833)	(3.133)	(2.753)	(2.115)	(0.896)
Observations	18	18	19	18	18	18	19	18
R-squared	0.622	0.628	0.430	0.417	0.556	0.563	0.309	0.318

Notes: Standard errors are reported in parentheses below coefficient estimates. Asterisks indicate statistical significance at the 1 percent (***), 5 percent (**), and 10 percent (*) levels, respectively.

TABLE 6-3. Taylor Rule Estimates (Ghana)

Model	(1.1) CPI + Output + Lag	(1.2) CPI + Output + Lag	(2) CPI + Lag	(3) CPI Only	(4.1) Output + Lag	(4.2) Output + Lag	(5.1) CPI + Output	(5.2) CPI + Output
CPI	0.272** (0.122)	0.261** (0.121)	0.279** (0.122)	0.562*** (0.114)			0.561*** (0.119)	0.553*** (0.117)
Output_Gap_HP	0.183 (0.189)				0.206 (0.212)		−0.014 (0.231)	
Output_Gap_Linear		0.176 (0.146)				0.214 (0.162)		0.113 (0.181)
Policy_Rate_Lag	0.577*** (0.165)	0.558*** (0.156)	0.525*** (0.156)		0.795*** (0.150)	0.765*** (0.137)		
Constant	5.290* (2.738)	5.755** (2.560)	6.191** (2.571)	13.98*** (1.280)	3.427 (2.931)	4.003 (2.708)	13.99*** (1.323)	14.06*** (1.309)
Observations	18	18	18	19	18	18	19	19
R-squared	0.749	0.758	0.733	0.586	0.661	0.677	0.586	0.596

Notes: Standard errors are reported in parentheses below coefficient estimates. Asterisks indicate statistical significance at the 1 percent (***), 5 percent (**), and 10 percent (*) levels, respectively.

TABLE 6-4. Taylor Rules with Exchange Rates (Estimates for Ghana)

Model	(6.1)	(6.2)	(7.1)	(7.2)	(8.1)	(8.2)	(9.1)	(9.2)
	CPI + Output + XR + Lag		CPI + Output + XR		CPI + XR + Lag		Output + XR	
CPI	0.371**	0.125	0.631***	0.433***	0.381***	0.122		
	(0.123)	(0.105)	(0.106)	(0.139)	(0.121)	(0.101)		
Output_Gap_HP	0.143	0.049	0.014	-0.154			-0.177	-0.377
	(0.174)	(0.151)	(0.198)	(0.239)			(0.347)	(0.287)
Policy_Rate_Lag	0.437**	0.641***			0.389**	0.630***		
	(0.168)	(0.129)			(0.156)	(0.120)		
AVG_FC_USD	0.005*		0.008**		0.005*		0.003	
	(0.003)		(0.003)		(0.003)		(0.005)	
Change_FC		0.138***		0.105		0.142***		0.199**
		(0.043)		(0.069)		(0.040)		(0.078)
Constant	3.096	2.698	6.988***	10.90***	3.733	2.883	17.91***	15.85***
	(2.408)	(2.034)	(2.172)	(1.957)	(2.254)	(1.887)	(2.080)	(1.446)
Observations	18	18	19	18	18	18	19	18
R-squared	0.805	0.862	0.715	0.598	0.795	0.861	0.040	0.318

Notes: Standard errors are reported in parentheses below coefficient estimates. Asterisks indicate statistical significance at the 1 percent (***), 5 percent (**), and 10 percent (*) levels, respectively.

TABLE 6-5. **Taylor Rule Estimates (WAEMU)**

Model	(1.1) CPI + Output + Lag	(1.2) CPI + Output + Lag	(2) CPI + Lag	(3) CPI Only	(4.1) Output + Lag	(4.2) Output + Lag	(5.1) CPI + Output	(5.2) CPI + Output
CPI	0.094*	0.110**	0.080	0.143*			0.158*	0.180**
	(0.051)	(0.051)	(0.052)	(0.080)			(0.077)	(0.070)
Output_Gap_HP	0.094				0.071		0.153	
	(0.063)				(0.067)		(0.097)	
Output_Gap_Linear		0.049*				0.029		0.094**
		(0.027)				(0.029)		(0.036)
Policy_Rate_Lag	0.552***	0.507***	0.554***		0.573***	0.548***		
	(0.137)	(0.135)	(0.143)		(0.148)	(0.150)		
Constant	2.262***	2.532***	2.174***	4.920***	1.785**	1.895**	4.995***	5.091***
	(0.654)	(0.660)	(0.679)	(0.349)	(0.652)	(0.664)	(0.337)	(0.305)
Observations	17	17	17	18	17	17	18	18
R-squared	0.632	0.656	0.570	0.167	0.535	0.532	0.286	0.431

Notes: Standard errors are reported in parentheses below coefficient estimates. Asterisks indicate statistical significance at the 1 percent (***), 5 percent (**), and 10 percent (*) levels, respectively.

TABLE 6-6. **Taylor Rules with Exchange Rates (Estimates for WAEMU)**

Model	(6.1) CPI + Output + XR + Lag	(6.2)	(7.1) CPI + Output + XR	(7.2)	(8.1) CPI + XR + Lag	(8.2)	(9.1) Output + XR	(9.2)
CPI	0.121** (0.048)	0.097* (0.053)	0.155** (0.053)	0.149* (0.079)	0.119** (0.047)	0.081 (0.054)		
Output_Gap_HP	0.046 (0.063)	0.096 (0.066)	0.010 (0.074)	0.152 (0.098)			−0.014 (0.090)	0.130 (0.105)
Policy_Rate_Lag	0.410** (0.145)	0.580*** (0.169)			0.389** (0.140)	0.571*** (0.176)		
AVG_FC_USD	0.025* (0.013)		0.046*** (0.011)		0.029** (0.012)		0.047*** (0.013)	
Change_FC		0.005 (0.015)		−0.016 (0.020)		0.003 (0.016)		−0.021 (0.021)
Constant	0.358 (0.889)	1.574* (0.740)	0.507 (0.841)	4.050*** (0.221)	0.155 (0.828)	1.623* (0.770)	0.804 (1.027)	4.355*** (0.164)
Observations	17	17	18	18	17	17	18	18
R-squared	0.718	0.635	0.691	0.319	0.706	0.571	0.498	0.144

Notes: Standard errors are reported in parentheses below coefficient estimates. Asterisks indicate statistical significance at the 1 percent (***), 5 percent (**), and 10 percent (*) levels, respectively.

ECOWAS SYNTHETIC TAYLOR RULE

The results from the Taylor estimations for Nigeria, Ghana, and WAEMU point to substantive differences in the determinants of the respective policy interest rates. This highlights the challenges involved in formulating a common monetary policy rule for ECOWAS.

One thought experiment we now turn to is to consider what the policy rate from an estimated Taylor rule would look like for ECOWAS as a whole. The variables that enter the Taylor rule specification are the same as in the previous exercises: the policy rate, the output gap, inflation, and the exchange rate. Each of these variables is now defined for the ECOWAS region as a whole. Aggregate variables are weighted using 2018 nominal GDP in U.S. dollars. For instance, ECOWAS inflation is measured as the weighted average of inflation in these three countries/areas, using nominal GDP in current U.S. dollars in 2018 as the weights. The Taylor rule estimation uses, as before, the deviation of inflation from a target rate of 6 percent. The ECOWAS output gap is calculated by first creating a weighted index of output, then detrending log output using either the Hodrick-Prescott filter or a linear time trend. Appendix D describes in further detail the sources and construction of these variables.

Table 6-7 shows that the coefficient on CPI inflation is significant in a couple of specifications but drops out when the lagged policy rate is included. Since the coefficient on inflation was significant in the estimations for Ghana and WAEMU, this result is presumably driven by Nigeria. The lagged policy rate enters with a significant and large coefficient in all specifications. The output gap enters with a negative coefficient in specification (5.2).

The next set of regressions explicitly includes exchange rates. Since there is no ECOWAS common currency, we created a synthetic exchange rate variable as a weighted average of the CFA franc, the Nigerian naira, and the Ghanaian cedi, weighted by 2018 nominal GDP in U.S. dollar terms. The estimates in table 6-8 show that neither the level nor the change in the artificial ECOWAS exchange rate enters significantly into any of the specifications.

SUMMARY

Table 6-9 summarizes selected Taylor rule models for ECOWAS, Ghana, Nigeria, and WAEMU, based on the regression fit and consistency of the co-

TABLE 6-7. Taylor Rule Estimates (ECOWAS)

Model	(1.1) CPI + Output + Lag	(1.2) CPI + Output + Lag	(2) CPI + Lag	(3) CPI Only	(4.1) Output + Lag	(4.2) Output + Lag	(5.1) CPI + Output	(5.2) CPI + Output
CPI	0.081 (0.167)	0.065 (0.162)	0.088 (0.159)	0.563*** (0.191)			0.402* (0.210)	0.363* (0.190)
Output_Gap_HP	−0.046 (0.190)				−0.062 (0.182)		−0.390 (0.249)	
Output_Gap_Linear		−0.091 (0.103)				−0.098 (0.098)		−0.285** (0.123)
Policy_Rate_Lag	0.597*** (0.152)	0.539*** (0.161)	0.609*** (0.139)		0.619*** (0.141)	0.555*** (0.151)		
Constant	3.855** (1.702)	4.600** (1.814)	3.670** (1.469)	8.767*** (0.981)	3.932** (1.647)	4.678** (1.748)	9.563*** (1.069)	9.714*** (0.961)
Observations	17	17	17	18	17	17	18	18
R-squared	0.643	0.662	0.642	0.351	0.637	0.658	0.442	0.522

Notes: Standard errors are reported in parentheses below coefficient estimates. Asterisks indicate statistical significance at the 1 percent (***), 5 percent (**), and 10 percent (*) levels, respectively.

TABLE 6-8. Taylor Rules with Exchange Rates (Estimates for ECOWAS)

Model	(6.1)	(6.2)	(7.1)	(7.2)	(8.1)	(8.2)	(9.1)	(9.2)
	CPI + Output + XR + Lag		CPI + Output + XR		CPI + XR + Lag		Output + XR	
CPI	0.073	0.084	0.390	0.409*	0.059	0.091		
	(0.158)	(0.175)	(0.224)	(0.219)	(0.155)	(0.167)		
Output_Gap_HP	0.191	-0.050	-0.421	-0.396			-0.698**	-0.623**
	(0.233)	(0.199)	(0.296)	(0.259)			(0.266)	(0.247)
Policy_Rate_Lag	0.647***	0.596***			0.601***	0.609***		
	(0.147)	(0.158)			(0.134)	(0.144)		
AVG_FC_USD	0.016		-0.003		0.011		-0.009	
	(0.010)		(0.014)		(0.008)		(0.015)	
Change_FC		-0.007		-0.015		-0.005		0.001
		(0.045)		(0.066)		(0.043)		(0.070)
Constant	0.340	3.382	7.729**	7.165***	2.241	3.685**	12.71***	11.35***
	(2.716)	(2.135)	(3.537)	(2.329)	(1.744)	(1.529)	(2.215)	(0.703)
Observations	17	17	18	18	17	17	18	18
R-squared	0.706	0.644	0.444	0.444	0.689	0.642	0.324	0.306

Notes: Standard errors are reported in parentheses below coefficient estimates. Asterisks indicate statistical significance at the 1 percent (***), 5 percent (**), and 10 percent (*) levels, respectively.

efficients across specifications. The policy rules for Ghana and Nigeria have similar sensitivities to CPI inflation and the lagged policy rate, though the exchange rate plays a significant role only for Ghana. Compared to these two countries, the WAEMU policy rate has a weaker association with inflation and a stronger association with the level of the exchange rate. The structure of Nigeria's economy clearly yields a very different Taylor rule than for the rest of ECOWAS. Consequently, the estimated Taylor rule for ECOWAS yields coefficients that are unstable across specifications, and are very different from those estimated for Ghana and WAEMU.

Figure 6-6 shows the fitted policy rates from the selected regressions and also the actual policy rates for Nigeria, Ghana, and WAEMU. The fitted rates track the actual rates reasonably well, although there are significant deviations between the two in the case of Nigeria, reflecting the poorer fit of the standard Taylor rule specifications for Nigeria.

Figure 6-7 shows the synthetic composite policy rate for ECOWAS and the fitted values from different models. The top panel shows that the model with CPI inflation alone has a relatively poor fit, which improves substantially once the lagged policy rate is included. The next two panels compare ECOWAS policy rates, fitted values from estimated Taylor rules, and the actual policy rates for Nigeria, Ghana, and WAEMU.

These figures highlight some key challenges in formulating a common set of monetary and exchange rate policies for ECOWAS. First, any policy rule for ECOWAS that takes into account relative country sizes will be dominated by economic conditions in Nigeria. Second, the differences in economic structures and effects of external shocks imply that—even if there is consensus among ECOWAS members in terms of the relative importance of inflation, output gaps, and exchange rate fluctuations in setting policy rates—the optimal policy rules look quite different for Nigeria than for WAEMU and Ghana. Third, and following from the second point, the desirable policy rate settings for Nigeria are likely to be quite different from those for WAEMU and Ghana, which could make it complicated to use a common exchange rate regime and monetary policy framework.

It is possible that the formation of a currency union will, over time, lead to a convergence of economic conditions across the member countries that reduces the inconsistency in desired policy settings. But the transition period could be long and create stresses within the zone.

TABLE 6-9. Selected Taylor Rule Models

| | ECOWAS | | Ghana | | Nigeria | WAEMU |
	Model (2)	Model (3)	Model (8.1)	Model (8.2)	Model (8.1)	Model (8.1)
CPI	0.088	0.563***	0.381***	0.122	0.318*	0.119**
AVG_FC_USD			0.005**			0.029**
Change_FC				0.142***		
Policy_Rate_Lag	0.609***		0.389**	0.630***	0.578***	0.389**
Constant	3.670**	8.767***	3.733	2.883	3.209	0.155
R-squared	0.642	0.351	0.795	0.861	0.555	0.706

Notes: Standard errors are reported in parentheses below coefficient estimates. Asterisks indicate statistical significance at the 1 percent (***), 5 percent (**), and 10 percent (*) levels, respectively.

FIGURE 6-6. **Fitted Curves for Major Member States**

A. Regression results—Ghana

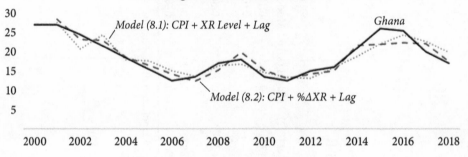

B. Regression results—Nigeria

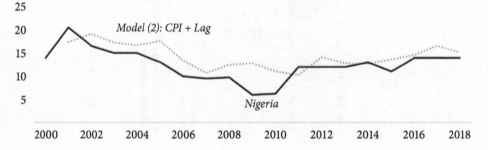

C. Regression results—WAEMU

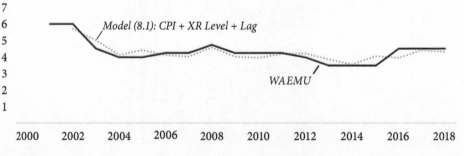

Source: Authors' calculations, based on estimates reported in table 6-9.

FIGURE 6-7. Fitted Curves for ECOWAS

A. ECOWAS regression results

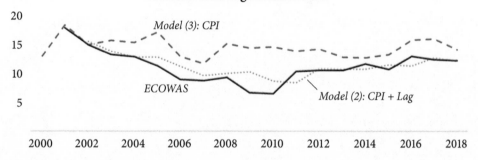

B. Policy rate comparison (1)

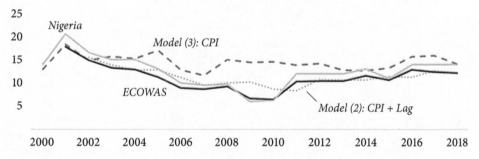

B. Policy rate comparison (2)

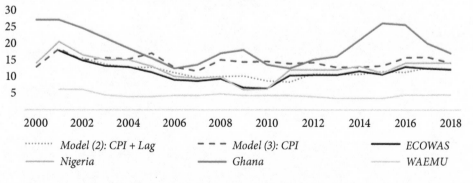

Source: Authors' calculations, based on estimates reported in table 6-9.

7

Institutional Framework, Policy Coordination

There are a number of significant operational challenges to combining into a currency union a set of countries that have disparate levels of economic development, different monetary policy frameworks, and fragmented factor markets. This chapter first reviews issues related to the harmonization of different monetary policy frameworks. Drawing on recent experiences of other currency unions such as the eurozone, the chapter will then provide a discussion of what other aspects of economic and financial union ECOWAS leaders should incorporate into their discussions.

HARMONIZATION FROM STARTING POINT OF DIFFERENT FRAMEWORKS

One of the key operational challenges is related to the harmonization of monetary policy across the zone. There is currently a wide variety of existing monetary arrangements among ECOWAS countries. Eight of the countries (Benin, Burkina Faso, Côte d'Ivoire, Guinea-Bissau, Mali, Niger, Senegal, and Togo) are part of the West African Economic and Monetary Union (WAEMU), which was formed in 1994. This union is part of the broader

CFA franc zone and has a currency that was initially pegged to the French franc and, since the advent of the euro, has been pegged to that currency.

Among the other countries, there are differences in the relative importance of various objectives of monetary policy as well as in practical aspects of monetary policy implementation. Nigeria, the largest economy in ECOWAS, has a flexible inflation targeting (IT) regime, wherein monetary policy is anchored by an inflation target but with some weight on output and employment. Ghana, the second-largest economy, has an independent central bank that also pursues a flexible IT regime. Even between such economies that have similar monetary frameworks in principle, there are important differences in operational aspects.

The Central Bank of Nigeria uses monetary aggregates as an intermediate target while the Bank of Ghana runs a more traditional IT regime by setting policy interest rates to achieve its inflation objective. The central banks of the remaining countries (other than those in WAEMU) have price stability—defined as low inflation—as the primary objective. However, some of these central banks—including those of Cabo Verde, the Gambia, and Liberia—also explicitly highlight exchange rate stability as an objective, on par with price stability.

There are also differences in the degree and nature of central bank independence among these countries. The central banks of Ghana, Sierra Leone, and the Gambia appear to have operational as well as statutory independence. As in the cases of independent central banks in many other emerging markets and developing economies, even these institutions set inflation targets in consultation with their governments. The central banks of Cabo Verde, Nigeria, and most of the others at a minimum have operational independence in achieving their objectives.

KEY INSTITUTIONAL ELEMENTS

The transition path to a common central bank for the zone will require a number of institutional and operational features to be decided in advance, particularly in order to build credibility for the monetary policy operations of the new central bank:

Monetary Policy Framework

One practical approach would be flexible inflation targeting, with a "leaning against the wind" component that involves central bank intervention to mitigate high levels of short-term volatility in foreign exchange markets without resisting longer-term directional changes in the exchange rate. The operating framework for implementing monetary policy will depend on the level of development and degree of integration of financial markets within the zone. This is a crucial determinant of the monetary policy transmission mechanism. In the absence of well-integrated financial markets, the operational tools of the common central bank would also be fragmented across countries, which could complicate the formulation and communication of monetary policy.

Definition of Inflation Target

It is necessary to determine an appropriate zone-wide price aggregate that is suitable as the inflation target. The issues to be resolved here include: (1) choosing the price index (for example, CPI or core CPI);[1] (2) determining the procedure for weighting inflation in different countries in order to arrive at a measure of zone-wide inflation; (3) setting the target level of inflation, which typically needs to be done in consultation with national governments; (4) clearly articulating whether the target is a point target, a band, or a ceiling; and (5) postulating whether monetary policy responses will be symmetric in response to positive and negative deviations from the target (or at different positions within the band).

Measurement of Economic Activity, Including
Slack in The Economy and Labor Markets

Construction of measures of overall economic slack, including measurement of output gaps and deviations of unemployment from the natural rate (or the non-accelerating inflation rate of unemployment), is challenging for even a single advanced economy. The challenges for developing countries and at the level of the zone are even greater, particularly since there appear to be some nontrivial conceptual differences across countries in the measurement and reporting of key variables.[2] There is also a risk to the political legitimacy of the currency union if measures of inflation and economic slack are dominated by two or three large economies.

Governance, Legitimacy, and Accountability

The decisionmaking structure of the zone's central bank will need to reflect representation of member countries, while being amenable to effective and timely policymaking without political interference. The processes for nominating and appointing members to the decisionmaking arm will need to be transparent and the body will need to be accountable to the entire zone.

Communication

The new central bank will need to pay particular attention to its communication and outreach strategies, especially in the initial stages, when it is working to build credibility with financial market participants. These are difficult challenges for any central bank, but specifically so for a new central bank that is trying to understand the transmission of monetary policy to financial and macroeconomic aggregates in the region.

ASPECTS OF BROADER ECONOMIC UNION

An important issue that ECOWAS leaders will need to address is what level of economic union is necessary to promote the stability of the monetary union. A full economic union, with a single fiscal policy and a unified banking system, is not on the cards in the foreseeable future.

A full economic union is certainly not essential for the successful operation of the monetary zone, but, in the absence of macroeconomic convergence and strong institutional frameworks, a partial union could create centrifugal stresses. These stresses could undermine the union if, for instance, different countries have different levels and growth rates of productivity in tandem with weak cross-border adjustment mechanisms, as noted earlier.

A fiscal union could allow for a more disciplined zone-wide approach to fiscal policy without being subject to national-level political considerations. But such a setup would perforce impinge on national prerogatives to set spending priorities and methods for financing them. A narrower but more pragmatic approach to unifying fiscal policy involves (1) mechanisms for disciplining each country's fiscal policy and (2) designing ex ante a mechanism for transferring fiscal resources across provinces in order to smooth out the effects of temporary, country-specific shocks. Designing a set of such rules in advance is important for the resilience of the union in difficult times.

Another issue is whether a banking union is essential, both in terms of ensuring financial stability and promoting the more effective transmission of the unified monetary policy throughout the zone.

The experiences of the eurozone are important for ECOWAS leaders to review carefully. The large net fiscal transfers to economically weaker countries in the zone created enormous stresses that posed the risk of tearing apart the zone. With fragmented banking regulation, financial system stresses in some of the periphery countries became an additional source of system-wide stress. The response to the eurozone debt crisis created what some authors have characterized as a "diabolic loop" between fiscal policy and the banking system in the affected countries. As output in some of these countries fell, putting stress on both the public finances and the banking system, the use of public money to recapitalize failing banks led to a self-reinforcing loop of rising interest rates, declines in economic activity, weakening of fiscal positions, and further stresses in the banking system.

One of the (many) lessons of the eurozone debt crisis is the need for harmonized banking regulation, especially of systemically important financial institutions (even those that may be systemically important for only their home countries rather than the entire zone).

Thus, at a minimum, it will be important for ECOWAS leaders to take a stand on how they will coordinate regulation of financial markets—including banks and nonbank financial institutions—in the proposed monetary zone.

HARMONIZED INSTITUTIONAL FRAMEWORK

A strong supporting institutional framework is needed at the level of the zone, in addition to harmonizing specific elements of institutions within each country. As preparation for the ECOWAS currency zone proceeds, it is essential to review progress toward institutional harmonization. Some of the relevant areas include:

- Harmonization of trade regimes and elimination of trade barriers within the zone

- Effective mechanism for gathering macroeconomic and other data; rapidly evaluating extent and reasons for deviations from agreed-upon criteria and robust, transparent framework for dealing with deviations

- Functioning of national coordinating committees and implementation of the multilateral surveillance mechanism

- Harmonized banking supervision and regulation that can take into account both micro and systemic risks, within specific countries and across the entire group; likewise, for nonbank financial institutions

- Harmonization of regulations concerning current account and capital account transactions

- Risk pooling mechanism among members in order to deal with external shocks (such as commodity price shocks) that may affect individual countries asymmetrically

- Regional payment system, with rapid settlement of cross-border transactions; integration into global payment systems

Appendix A provides a detailed description of the institutional architecture underpinning the eurozone. The appendix shows how many institutional elements are needed, ranging from managing monetary policy and financial regulation to harmonizing data and macroeconomic surveillance procedures, and that they have to work in harmony. The appendix also provides an idea of the timeline for the preparatory stages of initiating a complex currency union.

ROLE OF ANCHOR COUNTRY

An important consideration, particularly in light of the eurozone experience, is the relevance of a core country or a core group of countries for the governance and stability of a currency union. Germany accounts for 31 percent of the eurozone's GDP and 24 percent of its population. Broadening the core group to include Belgium, France, Germany, and the Netherlands yields GDP and population shares of 58 percent and 52 percent, respectively.[3] For comparison, as noted earlier, Nigeria accounts for 70 percent of GDP and 52 percent of the population in ECOWAS. Adding in the next two largest economies—Côte d'Ivoire and Ghana—these shares rise to 85 percent and 67 percent, respectively.

Germany is regarded as an important anchor of the eurozone's stability, particularly since it was perceived as a strong proponent of fiscal and monetary discipline even before EMU. As a relatively large and rich country within the zone, it has also provided significant transfers to the "periphery" countries, which are typically smaller and have lower per capita incomes. These transfers have taken place through the European Union budget and the cross-border interbank settlement system called TARGET2. Positive balances (claims) of a given country in the TARGET2 system represent gross claims of a country's central bank and commercial banks on the corresponding financial institutions of other countries that have negative balances (liabilities).[4]

These balances were small during the 2000s but mushroomed in the aftermath of the eurozone debt crisis. In principle, the large positive balances that Germany has in the TARGET2 system, offset by the large negative balances of many of the periphery economies such as Greece, Ireland, Italy, Portugal, and Spain are temporary and will eventually be settled by inter-country transfers in the opposite direction. In practice, however, the balances have grown persistently and continue to diverge.

Some scholars have argued that the implicit transfers through TARGET2 have served as a hidden mechanism through which Germany subsidizes other members of the eurozone and that these subsidies could end up becoming permanent.[5] This view has been forcefully rebutted by ECB researchers, who argue that the large and persistent TARGET2 balances reflect "cross-border payments that arise in the context of the APP [the ECB's asset purchase program] in an integrated euro area financial market and is not indicative of increased financial market stress, rising fragmentation, or unsustainable balance of payments developments" (see Eisenschmidt and others, 2017).[6] Whatever the correct interpretation might be, this discussion highlights the need to carefully evaluate the design of various direct and indirect transfer mechanisms, both from economic and political standpoints. This is particularly important from the standpoint of the core country.

Although the parallels with the eurozone are far from exact, it is worth considering the role that Nigeria might play as the dominant role in an ECOWAS currency union. One issue is whether Nigeria is prepared to make transfers to other countries in order to buffer them from external shocks, particularly since the other countries are unlikely to be able to offer insurance on a similar scale to an economy that is many times their size. Moreover, Nigeria might be even more constrained in its own policy responses to domestic and external shocks since the overall stability of the currency union could depend on the credibility and discipline of its policies. The same considerations are relevant if one regards the three largest ECOWAS economies as constituting the core. In short, asymmetries in the sizes and levels of development of the ECOWAS countries could create some additional challenges. A strong governance structure that keeps these potential cross-country tensions contained is therefore essential for a stable currency union.

ANCILLARY ISSUES

There are a number of other issues that are relevant for making growth in the region robust and sustainable, and for spreading the benefits of growth more evenly. Some of these issues are relevant for the economic progress of the region even independently of the goal of monetary union. These include regional financial market development and integration, especially as it relates to fixed-income securities markets (government and corporate bonds) and money markets. Another important priority is financial inclusion through traditional as well as new technologies, including mobile banking.

8

The Path Forward

An ECOWAS currency zone would be a major and ambitious undertaking, with many prospective benefits. It has the potential to improve trade and investment flows in the region, bring added discipline to the macroeconomic and structural policies of member countries, and enhance stability against external shocks. A currency union with a strong central bank can serve as an anchor for inflation expectations within the zone. A currency union can also serve as an external catalyst for labor and product market reforms in the member countries, since they would need adjustment mechanisms other than the exchange rate to respond to both domestic and external shocks. Such reforms can have significant positive welfare effects. In addition, a currency union can serve as an external disciplining device on fiscal policies.

But there are also significant costs, operational challenges, and transitional risks. With member countries having widely varying production and economic structures, the loss of an adjustment mechanism—in the form of an independent currency and monetary policy—puts a significant burden on other policies.

The academic literature on optimum currency areas has identified a number of key criteria for a successful currency union, including the symmetry (similarity) of shocks across countries, mobility of factors of production, openness to trade and finance, and degree of economic diversification.

Based on these criteria, the members of ECOWAS do not fulfill the prerequisites for a currency union.

There are considerable differences in the structures of their economies. Moreover, many of them are not well diversified and retain a high degree of reliance on the primary sector for generating GDP and, especially, for their exports. There is limited co-movement of GDP growth and inflation across ECOWAS countries. Terms-of-trade shocks are a key driver of economic fluctuations in most ECOWAS countries, accounting for a significant share of the variation in GDP growth and inflation. However, these shocks are not symmetric across the region, with a particularly strong asymmetry between the terms-of-trade shocks faced by Nigeria and WAEMU.

Given these circumstances, other adjustment mechanisms are essential for an ECOWAS currency union's ability to withstand aggregate shocks as well as shocks that affect countries asymmetrically. These mechanisms include (1) flexible product and labor markets, (2) labor mobility across countries and wage flexibility within countries, (3) mechanisms for sharing risk, and (4) a fiscal transfer system.

Initial conditions and congruence of macroeconomic conjunctures are also important for a successful currency union. ECOWAS leaders have determined a set of criteria—four main indicators and two ancillary ones—to assess macroeconomic convergence. Progress on meeting these criteria has been mixed. There are significant risks to moving forward with a monetary union if the agreed-upon criteria are not met by all countries. This could reduce the credibility of the currency zone and would, at the outset, undermine the enforcement mechanisms intended to ensure consistency of economic policies across member countries. Moreover, as the world economy becomes more interconnected through trade and financial linkages, the vulnerability of ECOWAS member countries to external demand and financing shocks might need to be incorporated into a set of additional convergence criteria.

Based on the characteristics of ECOWAS economies, especially the high degree of exposure to terms of trade and other external shocks, a flexible exchange rate regime, in tandem with a nominal anchor provided by an inflation targeting regime, appears to be a better option than a fixed exchange rate. This combination would help secure stability in the form of low inflation, with the flexible exchange rate providing a buffer against external shocks. Welfare calculations using a simple dynamic general equilibrium model bolster this conclusion. This framework could be supplemented with a "leaning against the wind" option. This option entails limiting short-term exchange rate volatility while not fundamentally resisting, through foreign exchange market intervention, market pressures pushing the currency in one direction or the other.

For all its potential benefits, such a regime is not without risks. A more flexible exchange rate and open capital account can make a developing economy more vulnerable to global financial cycles, including monetary policy spillovers from advanced economies that can trigger capital flow volatility. Exchange rate volatility can impose stresses on public finances and corporate balance sheets in the presence of significant levels of foreign currency debt. Fiscal dominance can also threaten price stability in the absence of a trusted and hard nominal anchor such as a fixed exchange rate. Both of these are relevant considerations given that most ECOWAS countries have high levels of public debt and some of them have significant levels of foreign currency external debt.

An analysis of how a common ECOWAS currency regime and monetary policy framework might function shows that, based on the high degree of divergence in current practices, it will be essential but challenging to first develop a consensus among ECOWAS members about the relative importance of variables such as inflation, output gaps, and exchange rate fluctuations in setting policy rates. Even with a consensus on these issues, there could be difficulties in formulating a common set of monetary and exchange rate policies for ECOWAS. First, any policy rule for ECOWAS that takes into account relative country sizes will be dominated by economic conditions in Nigeria. Second, the differences in economic structures and effects of external shocks imply that optimal policy rules look quite different for Nigeria than for WAEMU and Ghana. Third, and following from the second point, the desirable policy rate settings for Nigeria are likely to be quite different from those for WAEMU and Ghana, which could make it complicated to use a common exchange rate regime and monetary policy framework.

There are a number of significant operational challenges to combining into a union a set of countries that have disparate levels of economic development, different monetary policy frameworks, and fragmented factor markets. The economic dominance of Nigeria—by far the largest country in the proposed currency zone in terms of both GDP and population—and its inevitable role as an anchor country pose additional challenges. For Nigeria, in particular, there is a complex set of considerations related to its size and likely role as anchor country in an ECOWAS currency union. Nigeria's economy could certainly benefit from greater trade and financial integration with other ECOWAS countries, but at the potential cost of having to calibrate some of its policy settings to economic conditions in the region rather than its own economy.

For a smaller country, such as Senegal, there is a complex set of considerations related to its membership of an existing currency union and how that union would integrate into a larger currency union that is dominated by two countries—Nigeria and Ghana. Senegal's economy could certainly benefit from greater trade and financial integration with those and other ECOWAS countries, but at the potential cost of having policy settings within ECOWAS calibrated more to the economic needs of those large economies.

The substantial differences across ECOWAS countries in terms of their present exchange rate and monetary arrangements could create some transitional risks. Moreover, the disparities in capital account openness could complicate the management of whatever exchange rate regime is chosen for the eventual currency union.

ALTERNATIVES TO A COMMON CURRENCY

It is also worth considering if there are alternative approaches that could generate similar benefits in terms of greater regional trade and financial integration. For instance, there is now an extensive set of trade and financial arrangements among Asian countries, while each of them retains monetary policy autonomy. Regional risk-sharing mechanisms, such as the Chiang Mai Initiative, have taken on some of the proposed functions of the currency union. Similarly, as a catalyst for regional financial market development, the Asian Bond Fund Initiative became a substitute for more direct financial integration through a currency union. Whether such regional trade and financial agreements have positive effects of the same magnitude as a currency union on trade flows and broader economic integration remains an open question.

In light of Asia's approach and in view of progress on the African Continental Free Trade Area, it is worth considering if a set of arrangements to promote trade and financial integration would serve as a useful—and perhaps even necessary—precursor to a more durable and resilient ECOWAS currency union. It should be recognized that ECOWAS has already made progress in this dimension. Initiatives include the ECOWAS Trade Liberalization Scheme (ETLS) and the Common External Tariff (CET) that was introduced in 2015. Moreover, national authorities are taking measures at the country level, complemented by ongoing work at the regional level, to remove obstacles to freer trade flows. Such measures will have a positive effect on the preparedness of the region for a possible currency union.[1]

There are many residual issues that will need to be considered carefully as ECOWAS members contemplate the formation of a currency union. These include: Does the existence of a currency union among two-thirds of the members of ECOWAS simplify or complicate the process of creating a larger currency union? How can a disparate set of monetary policy frameworks converge to a unified one managed by a zone-wide central bank? Is there a way to broaden the currency union gradually, adding countries when they meet various convergence criteria, rather than moving to a full-fledged ECOWAS currency union in one go? What would determine the optimal timing, from the perspective of global developments, to move forward with the currency union? In addition to addressing these questions and before proceeding with monetary union, it will be important for ECOWAS member countries to make sure the union can remain resilient when global and regional conditions turn difficult.

Indeed, the coronavirus pandemic has highlighted some of these challenges, which would inevitably complicate the transition to a currency union. The pandemic, and the ensuing global recession, have resulted in a difficult global economic and financial environment. These are putting stresses on economies around the world, but particularly on emerging and developing economies. In the immediate aftermath of the coronavirus outbreak, there was a sharp reversal of capital flows from all emerging and developing economies. This has complicated financing of current account deficits and put pressure on external inflows into developing countries around the world, and the ECOWAS region is no exception. To add to these challenges, the sharp fall in oil prices, which could prove persistent if global demand takes a long time to recover, could strain Nigeria's public finances and macroeconomic position. As highlighted in this book, such sharp fluctuations in oil prices are likely to lead to divergence of macroeconomic positions of countries in the zone, with divergences in pass-through effects of oil prices to domestic inflation posing particular challenges.

There is, of course, a multitude of other economic and geopolitical risks that could affect world growth and financial markets in the years to come. Some of these risks could expose macroeconomic fissures within the zone, particularly if ECOWAS countries embark on monetary union before the convergence criteria and other conditions essential for a resilient union are met. Hence, before ECOWAS member countries proceed with the currency union, it will be important for them to redouble efforts to strengthen their macroeconomic and institutional frameworks to ensure the union remains resilient even when global and regional conditions turn difficult.

If ECOWAS leaders can find the resolve to implement these reforms, then a single currency could play a helpful role in attaining this region's full potential by removing trade and monetary barriers, reducing transaction costs, and boosting economic activity. This will not only raise the living standards of people in the region but could serve as a unifying factor and a means toward social and political integration.

The manner in which ECOWAS leaders make progress toward greater integration in the region could have broader implications for the African continent as a whole. The COVID-19 pandemic has reignited the discussion across Africa about monetary instruments to deal with the crisis and is likely to bring with it a renewed call for an African Monetary Fund as a first line of defense against global shocks. The experience of the ECOWAS region could provide useful lessons were efforts undertaken to create such an agency.

APPENDIX A

Comparing and Contrasting Asia's and Europe's Approaches to Economic Integration

REGIONAL TRADE ARRANGEMENTS

Association of Southeast Asian Nations (ASEAN, 1967). A regional organization that now includes Indonesia, Malaysia, the Philippines, Singapore, Thailand, Negara Brunei Darussalam, Vietnam, Laos, Myanmar, and Cambodia (five original members listed first; rest listed in the order they joined). In 1992, ASEAN implemented the ASEAN Free Trade Area (AFTA). Unlike the EU, the AFTA agreement does not set common external tariffs on imports. Rather, it reduces and eliminates intra-regional tariffs within ASEAN through the Common Effective Preferential Tariff (CEPT) scheme. In 2010, ASEAN countries signed the Trade in Goods Agreement to enhance the CEPT scheme.[1] ASEAN has successfully established ASEAN Plus Free Trade Agreements (FTAs) with China, Japan, Korea, Australia–New Zealand, and India.

Asia-Pacific Trade Agreement (1975). A preferential trade arrangement (formerly known as the Bangkok Agreement) that includes China, Bangladesh, India, Laos, South Korea, and Sri Lanka. After the latest round of negotiations, participating states agreed to provide at least 33 percent tariff concessions for over ten thousand products covered by the agreement, as well as to implement the Rules of Origin.[2]

Comprehensive and Progressive Agreement for Trans-Pacific Partnership (2018). A free trade agreement signed in March 2018 by eleven Asia-Pacific countries (Australia, Brunei Darussalam, Canada, Chile, Japan, Malaysia, Mexico, New Zealand, Peru, Singapore, and Vietnam). This agreement, which took the place of the Trans-Pacific Partnership, covers labor and environmental standards, intellectual property, e-commerce, and government procurement.

Regional Free Trade Agreements. So far, twenty-two East Asian intra-regional FTAs and eight West Asian intra-regional FTAs have entered into force. These agreements include the AFTA agreement, the ASEAN Plus FTAs, the South Asian Free Trade Area (SAFTA) agreement, and other bilateral FTAs. In addition, eleven of the Asian countries are Preferential Trade Agreement providers.

Regional Comprehensive Economic Partnership. A proposed ASEAN-centered regional free trade proposal, which includes ten ASEAN countries, as well as Australia, China, India, Japan, South Korea, and New Zealand. Its negotiations cover a broad range of issues such as trade, investment, economic and technical cooperation, intellectual property, competition, dispute settlement, e-commerce, and small and medium enterprises. The most recent round of negotiations (the twenty-second round) was held in Singapore from April 28 to May 8, 2018.

REGIONAL RISK-SHARING ARRANGEMENTS

Chiang Mai Initiative (CMI). In 2000, five ASEAN states (Indonesia, Malaysia, the Philippines, Singapore, and Thailand), together with China, Korea, and Japan, established the CMI to strengthen the cooperative frameworks among their central banks and monetary authorities. The initiative involved a network of bilateral swap and repurchase agreement facilities among members. The grand total of CMI commitments exceeded US$39 billion (with zero paid-in capital), and sixteen bilateral swap agreements were signed under the initiative.

Chiang Mai Initiative Multilateralization (CMIM). In 2010, the ASEAN+3 (with Hong Kong) multilateralized the CMI into a single contractual agreement to address balance of payments and short-term liquidity difficulties in the region, as well as to supplement existing international financial arrangements. Other facilities under CMIM include CMIM-PL for crisis prevention, CMIM-SF for crisis resolution, and the ASEAN+3 Macroeconomic Research Office (AMRO) for regional surveillance. In 2014, CMIM's commitment doubled to US$240 billion from its initial arrangement (with zero paid-in capital).

Cross-Border Collateral Arrangements (CBCAs). After the 2008 global financial crisis, a number of CBCAs were established among Asian countries to manage liquidity risk and to cope with new concerns arising from increasing intraregional banking.

Southeast Asia Disaster Risk Insurance Facility (SEADRIF). SEADRIF is a "regional catastrophe risk pool to provide rapid response financing in the immediate aftermath of a disaster." In May 2017, the governments of Cambodia, Laos, Myanmar, and Japan signed a memorandum of understanding (MoU) to develop the program. The program was officially announced in May 2018 (when Singapore also joined) and commenced operation in 2019.

REGIONAL FINANCIAL DEVELOPMENT AND INTEGRATION

Asian Bond Fund 1 (ABF1). In 2003, the eleven central banks of Executives' Meeting of East Asia and Pacific (EMEAP) launched the Asian Bond Fund (ABF) Initiative to "broaden and deepen regional and domestic bond markets in Asia."[3] The first stage of ABF (ABF1), from 2003 to 2004, pooled US$1 billion from the eleven EMEAP central banks to invest in dollar bonds issued by sovereign and quasi-sovereign borrowers in eight EMEAP markets (other than Australia, Japan, and New Zealand).

Asian Bond Fund 2 (ABF2). At the end of 2004, the second stage of ABF (ABF2) was launched to "provide a low-cost and efficient product in the form of passively managed bond funds, as well as to catalyze market and regulatory reforms at both regional and domestic levels." ABF2 is comprised of two phases: (i) US$2 billion investment into local currency-denominated bonds in eight EMEAP markets (other than Australia, Japan, and New Zealand) via the nine ABF2 funds, and (ii) opening up of the nine funds to public investment.[4] By 2011, both phases had been completed, and the size of ABF2 investment grew from the initial US$2 billion to about US$4 billion. In 2016, ABF1 was closed and the funds were transferred into ABF2.

Asian Bond Markets Initiative (ABMI). ABMI was launched by ASEAN+3 in 2002 to strengthen financial stability and reduce the region's vulnerability to sudden reversals of capital inflows. In 2012, ASEAN+3 officials launched guarantee operations under the Credit Guarantee and Investment Facility (CGIF). CGIF's guarantee capacity has been raised from US$700 million to US$1.75 billion with a leverage ratio of 1:2.5. As of March 2017, CGIF had issued seventeen credit guarantees (cumulatively valued at US$1.06 billion) for bonds issued in eight ASEAN member countries. The CGIF board also recently approved three additional guarantees amounting to US$310 million.

Asian Development Bank (ADB). Launched in early 1966, the ADB now has sixty-seven members, forty-eight of which are from the Asia and Pacific region. The ADB's main mission is to "help its developing member countries reduce poverty and improve the quality of life of their people," by providing loans, technical assistance, grants, and equity investments. In 2016, the ADB's total capital was US$143 billion (US$7 billion paid-in; US$136 billion callable).

Asian Infrastructure Investment Bank (AIIB). The AIIB was established in 2016 and had eighty-seven members as of June 2017. It is a China-led multilateral development bank that aims to improve social and economic outcomes in Asia and beyond, by offering sovereign and non-sovereign financing for projects in sustainable infrastructure and other productive sectors. AIIB's total capital was US$95 billion (US$19 billion paid-in capital) at the end of 2017. So far, AIIB has approved US$4 billion worth of investments in infrastructure projects.

REGIONAL SURVEILLANCE

ASEAN+3 Macroeconomic Research Office (AMRO). AMRO was initially established in 2011 as a surveillance unit of CMIM by ASEAN+3 (with Hong Kong SAR). In 2016, it was transformed into an international organization to better support the region's macroeconomic and financial stability. Its major functions are conducting macroeconomic surveillance, supporting the implementation of CMIM, and providing technical assistance to members. The organization is governed by an executive committee, an advisory panel, and a director who appoints his/her own staff. Member states are represented in AMRO through the executive committee, which consists of twenty-seven deputies, including one financial deputy and one central bank deputy from each member (with the exception of Hong Kong SAR). The executive committee appoints both the director and the members of advisory panel.

REGIONAL DEVELOPMENT PROGRAMS

Greater Mekong Subregion (GMS) Economic Cooperation Program. The GMS comprises Cambodia, China (specifically Yunnan Province and Guangxi Zhuang Autonomous Region), Laos, Myanmar, Thailand, and Vietnam. In 1992, with assistance from the ADB, these six countries entered into a program of subregional economic cooperation. The GMS program supports the implementation of high-priority projects in agriculture, energy, environment, health and human resource development, ICT, tourism, transport, transport and trade facilitation, and urban development. As of 2016, GMS projects have received US$19 billion in total.

Central Asia Regional Economic Cooperation (CAREC) Program. The CAREC program is a partnership of eleven countries (Afghanistan, Azerbaijan, China, Georgia, Kazakhstan, Kyrgyz Republic, Mongolia, Pakistan, Tajikistan, Turkmenistan, and Uzbekistan), supported by six multilateral institutions. Since its inception in 2001, CAREC has mobilized more than US$32 billion worth of investments for 185 regional development projects in transportation, energy, and trade sectors.

South Asia Subregional Economic Cooperation (SASEC) Initiative. This program brings together Bangladesh, Bhutan, India, Maldives, Myanmar, Nepal, and Sri Lanka in a project-based partnership that aims to promote regional prosperity, improve economic opportunities, and build a better quality of life for the people of the subregion. Since its establishment in 2001, SASEC has implemented forty-nine ADB-financed investment projects, worth more than US$11 billion, in transport, trade facilitation, energy, and economic corridor sectors.

THE EUROZONE: INSTITUTIONAL ARRANGEMENTS AND STAGES OF ECONOMIC AND MONETARY UNION

Stage One (July 1, 1990):
- Complete freedom for cross-border capital transactions
- Increased co-operation between central banks
- Free use of the ECU (European Currency Unit)
- Improvement of economic convergence

Stage Two (January 1, 1994):
- Establishment of the European Monetary Institute (EMI)
- Ban on the granting of central bank credit
- Increased coordination of monetary policies
- Strengthening of economic convergence
- Process leading to the independence of the national central banks, to be completed, at the latest, by the date of establishment of the European System of Central Banks
- Preparatory work for Stage Three

Stage Three (January 1, 1999):
- Irrevocable fixing of conversion rates
- Introduction of the euro
- Conduct of the single monetary policy by the European System of Central Banks
- Entry into effect of the intra-EU exchange rate mechanism (ERM II)
- Entry into force of the Stability and Growth Pact

Eleven members at commencement of eurozone: Austria, Belgium, Finland, France, Germany, Ireland, Italy, Luxembourg, the Netherlands, Portugal, and Spain.

Additional eight members: Greece (2001); Slovenia (2007); Cyprus, Malta (2008); Slovakia (2009); Estonia (2011); Latvia (2014); Lithuania (2015).

On the day each country joined the euro area, its central bank automatically became part of the Eurosystem.

Committee of Governors (1964–94)

The committee of governors of the central banks of the member states of the European Economic Community had played an increasingly important role in monetary cooperation since its creation in May 1964. The committee was given additional responsibilities through a European Council Decision dated March 12, 1990. The new tasks included holding consultations on, and promoting the coordination of, the monetary policies of the member states, with the aim of achieving price stability.

The European Monetary Institute (1994–98)

The European Monetary Institute (EMI) was established on January 1, 1994. Its establishment marked the start of the second stage of EMU and superseded the committee of governors. The EMI had no responsibility for the conduct of monetary policy in the European Union—this remained the preserve of the national authorities—nor had it any competence for carrying out foreign exchange intervention.

The two main tasks of the EMI:

- To strengthen central bank cooperation and monetary policy coordination

- To make the preparations required for the establishment of the European System of Central Banks (ESCB), for the conduct of the single monetary policy, and for the creation of a single currency in the third stage

To this end, the EMI provided a forum for consultation and for an exchange of views and information on policy issues, and it specified the regulatory, organizational, and logistical framework necessary for the ESCB to perform its tasks in Stage Three. The EMI was given the task of carrying out preparatory work on the future monetary and exchange rate relationships between the euro area and other EU countries. In December 1996, the EMI presented its report to the European Council, which formed the basis of a Resolution of the European Council on the Principles and Fundamental Elements of the New Exchange Rate Mechanism (ERM II), which was adopted in June 1997. In December 1996, the EMI also presented to the European Council, and subsequently to the public, the selected design series for the euro banknotes to be put into circulation on January 1, 2002.

On May 25, 1998, the governments of the eleven participating member states appointed the president, the vice-president, and the four other members of the executive board of the ECB. Their appointment took effect from June 1, 1998, and marked the establishment of the ECB. The ECB and the national central banks of the participating member states constitute the Eurosystem, which formulates and defines the single monetary policy in Stage Three of EMU.

With the establishment of the ECB on June 1, 1998, the EMI had completed its tasks and was terminated.

European Central Bank (1998–present)

The main functions of the ECB are as follows:[5]

- Set interest rates to control money supply and inflation.
- Manage the eurozone's foreign currency reserves and balance exchange rates.
- Ensure that financial markets and institutions are well supervised by national authorities and that payment systems work well.
- Ensure the safety and soundness of the European banking system.
- Authorize production of euro banknotes by eurozone countries.
- Monitor price trends and assess risks to price stability.

The structure of the ECB is as follows:[6]

- The main decisionmaking body is the Governing Council, which is comprised of:
  - Six members of the executive board (EB)
  - The governors of the national central banks (NCBs) of the nineteen euro-area countries
- The executive board has six members, who are appointed by the European Council for a nonrenewable term of eight years.
- The General Council is comprised of:
  - The president and the vice-president of the ECB and the governors of the NCBs of the twenty-eight EU member states
- The Supervisory Board (SB) is comprised of:
  - The chair, who is appointed for a nonrenewable term of five years
  - The vice-chair, who is chosen from among the members of the ECB's executive board

- Four ECB representatives
- Representatives of national supervisors

The Governing Council usually meets twice a month to design guidelines facilitating ECB and Eurosystem's tasks, formulate monetary policies, and adopt the general framework for making supervisory decisions.

The EB implements monetary policies following the guidelines and decisions made by the Governing Council, does the daily administration of the ECB, and wields delegated powers, including some regulatory powers.

European Commission (1958)

The European Commission (EC) is a European Union institution. Its functions are as follows:[7]

- Proposing laws to the European Parliament and Council of the European Union
- Helping member countries implement EU legislation
- Managing the EU's budget and allocating funding
- Together with the Court of Justice, ensuring that EU law is complied with
- Representing the EU outside Europe together with the EU's diplomatic service, the European External Action Service

Eurostat (1953)

Eurostat is the only provider of statistics at European level. It is one of the directorates-general of the European Commission.[8] Eurostat does not collect data, which is done by statistical authorities in member states. They verify and analyze national data and send them to Eurostat. Eurostat consolidates the data and ensures comparability, using a harmonized methodology.

European System of Financial Supervision (ESFS, 2010)

The ESFS contains three European Supervisory Authorities (ESAs), the European Systemic Risk Board (ESRB), and national supervisors. It aims to ensure consistent and appropriate financial supervision throughout the EU. The ESRB is responsible for macro-prudential supervision.[9]

The ESAs have responsibility for micro-prudential supervision, which covers individual institutions, such as banks, insurance companies, and pension funds. The ESAs include the European Banking Authority, European Insurance and Occupational Pensions Authority, and European Securities and Markets Authority, all of which commenced operation in January 2011.

TARGET2

TARGET2 is a platform for processing large-value payments and is used by both central banks and commercial banks to process payments in euro. The platform is owned and managed by the Eurosystem.[10]

TREATIES AND ACCORDS UNDERPINNING THE EMU

The Treaty on European Union was agreed in December 1991 and signed in Maastricht on February 7, 1992. After some delays in the ratification process, the treaty came into force on November 1, 1993. The Maastricht Treaty, officially known as the Treaty on European Union, laid the foundations for a single currency and significantly expanded cooperation between European countries in a number of new areas:

- European citizenship was created, allowing citizens to reside in and move freely between member states.

- A common foreign and security policy was established.

- Closer cooperation between police and the judiciary in criminal matters was agreed.

The treaty also set out the timeline for the introduction of the single currency and the convergence criteria. European leaders took additional steps to promote further integration:

- The Stability and Growth Pact (1997) was agreed to ensure that countries followed sound budgetary policies.

- The European Stability Mechanism was established to provide financial assistance to euro area countries experiencing or threatened by severe financing problems.

- The Single Supervisory Mechanism and the Single Resolution Board were created after the financial crisis to make the European banking system safer, as well as to increase financial integration and stability.

STABILITY AND GROWTH PACT

In order to complement and to specify the treaty provisions on EMU, the European Council adopted the Stability and Growth Pact in June 1997. The pact aims to ensure budgetary discipline in respect of EMU. It underwent reforms in 2005 and 2011.

The Preventive Arm

- The definition of the medium-term budgetary objective. Each country makes its own country-specific medium-term objective (MTO), which will be assessed by the EU Council instead of required to target close to balance or in surplus. However, the upper limit for MTO should be 3 percent deficit of GDP.

- The adjustment path to the medium-term objective. Member states can take steps to achieve their MTOs over the cycle. Euro area and ERM II member states should, as a benchmark, pursue an annual adjustment in cyclically adjusted terms, net of one-off and temporary measures, of 0.5 percent of GDP.

- Taking into account structural reforms. Member states are allowed a temporary deviation from the MTO if they are undertaking structural reforms. The upper limit will be preserved at all times.

The Corrective Arm

- The modification of the definition of a "severe economic downturn"[11]

- Specification of the "other relevant factors" when considering the initiation of an Excessive Deficit Procedure[12]

- Extension of procedural deadlines

- Extension of the deadlines for the correction of excessive deficits[13]

- Unexpected adverse events and repeated recommendations or notices

- Increasing the focus on debt and sustainability, but no quantitative definition has been made

APPENDIX B

Macroeconomic Convergence Criteria for Existing Monetary/Currency Unions

West African Economic and Monetary Union (UEMOA, 1994)[1]

Members: Benin, Bissau Guinea, Burkina Faso, Ivory Coast, Mali, Niger, Senegal, and Togo.

Primary Criteria:

- Annual average inflation rate ≤ 3 percent
- Budget deficit to GDP ratio ≤ 3 percent
- Ratio of total public debt to GDP ≤ 70 percent

Secondary Criteria:

- Tax revenue (excluding oil revenues) to GDP ratio ≥ 17 percent
- Ratio of wages and salaries to total tax revenue ratio ≤ 35 percent

Central African Economic and Monetary Community (CEMAC, 1999)[2]

Members: Cameroon, Central African Republic, Chad, Republic of Congo, Equatorial Guinea, and Gabon.

2001 Benchmarks:

- Annual average inflation rate ≤ 3 percent
- Basic fiscal balance ≥ 0[3]

- Ratio of total public debt to GDP ≤ 70 percent

- Tax revenue (excluding oil revenues) to GDP ratio ≥ 20 percent

- Wages and salaries to tax revenue ratio ≤ 35 percent

- Non-accumulation of arrears

2016 Revised Benchmarks:

- Three-year average inflation rate ≤ 3 percent

- Budget deficit to GDP ratio ≤ 1.5 percent[4]

- Ratio of total public debt to GDP ≤ 70 percent

- Tax revenue (excluding oil revenues) to GDP ratio ≥ 17 percent

- Wages and salaries to total revenue ratio ≤ 35 percent

- Ratio of capital expenditure to GDP ≥ 20 percent

- Real GDP growth rate ≥ 7 percent

- Non-accumulation of arrears

Eurozone (1999)[5]

Members: Austria, Belgium, Cyprus, Estonia, Finland, France, Germany, Greece, Ireland, Italy, Latvia, Lithuania, Luxembourg, Malta, the Netherlands, Portugal, Slovakia, Slovenia, and Spain.

Convergence Criteria for Initial Entry into EMU:

- *Price stability:* CPI inflation ≤ 1.5 percentage points above the rate of the three best performing member states

- *Sound public finances:* Government deficit ≤ 3 percent of GDP

- *Sustainable public finances:* Government debt ≤ 60 percent of GDP

- *Durability of convergence:* Long-term interest rate ≤ 2 percentage points above the rate of the three best performing member states in terms of price stability

- *Exchange rate stability:* Participation in ERM II for at least two years without severe tensions (measured as deviations from a central rate)

Institutional Arrangements:

- No monetary financing

- No privileged access to financial institutions

- No bailout clause

Fiscal Rules:
- Budget deficit to GDP ratio ≤ 3 percent
- Ratio of total public debt to GDP ≤ 60 percent

Sanctions:
- Failure to meet fiscal criteria and to take effective actions to correct deviations from those criteria may result in penalties amounting to 0.2 percent of GDP

- Assistance from the European Structural and Investment Funds may be suspended temporarily

- An annually variable component for continued noncompliance

Common Monetary Area (CMA, 1986)

Members: South Africa, Namibia, Lesotho, and Swaziland.
- There are no explicit fiscal rules for this currency union

Southern African Development Community (SADC, 1992)[6]

Members: Angola, Botswana, DR Congo, Lesotho, Madagascar, Malawi, Mauritius, Mozambique, Namibia, Seychelles, South Africa, Swaziland, Tanzania, Zambia, and Zimbabwe.
- Annual average inflation rate ≤ 10 percent by 2008, ≤ 5 percent by 2012, and ≤ 3 percent by 2018
- Budget deficit to GDP ratio (excluding grants) ≤ 5 percent by 2008 and between 2 percent and 4 percent by 2012
- Central bank credit to the government ≤ 10 percent of previous year's tax revenue by 2008 and ≤ 5 percent by 2015
- Ratio of total public debt to GDP ≤ 60 percent by 2008
- Gross external reserves ≥ 3 months of imports by 2008 and ≥ 6 months of imports by 2012
- Saving to GDP ≥ 25 percent by 2008 and ≥ 30 percent by 2012
- Domestic investment to GDP ≥ 30 percent by 2008

Eastern Caribbean Currency Union (ECCU, 1981)[7]

Members: Anguilla, Antigua and Barbuda, Dominica, Grenada, Montserrat, Saint Kitts and Nevis, Saint Lucia, Saint Vincent, and the Grenadines.

- The ECCU public debt target provides its member countries with a long-term anchor for their fiscal policies but offers no short-term operational guidance to achieve this goal; its members have their own fiscal rules
- Ratio of total public debt to GDP ≤ 60 percent
- Budget deficit to GDP ratio ≤ 3 percent
- The deficit target was abandoned in 2006 for lack of compliance, and in 2015 the 2020 deadline for the public debt target was extended to 2030

APPENDIX C

General Equilibrium Analysis of Alternative Exchange Rate and Monetary Policy Regimes

An important consideration in choosing from among alternative exchange rate and monetary policy regimes is an evaluation of their welfare effects in the face of different shocks. This section describes a dynamic stochastic general equilibrium model (DSGE) that can provide an explicit set of welfare calculations to address this question. Such a model can, of course, capture only a few key elements of an economy. Any results from such a model should, therefore, be taken as suggestive and be interpreted with considerable caution. These caveats are particularly relevant for developing economies, where markets are far from complete, credit constraints and other financial frictions abound, and price and wage formation do not necessarily conform to the assumptions of traditional economic models. These factors can have a substantial impact on the implementation and transmission of monetary policy.

The model developed in this appendix tries to capture some key features of developing economies. It features two sectors, one that produces tradable goods and the other that produces non-tradable goods. This feature is important for characterizing real exchange rate fluctuations (the real exchange rate is the relative price of non-tradables to tradables) and incorporates nominal price rigidities as well as financial frictions, in the form of liquidity constraints on a certain fraction of households in the economy. These constraints are a pervasive feature of developing economies and can have a significant impact on the transmission of nominal and real shocks.

Some of the key elements of the model are sketched out below. Further details about the model and solution techniques can be found in Anand, Prasad, and Zhang (2015) and Prasad and Zhang (2015).[1]

Main Elements of the Model

- Two sectors: tradable goods and non-tradable goods sector. Fraction of households working in the tradable sector is λ.

- Prices of traded goods: set in international markets in foreign currency; prices of non-traded goods set by monopolistically competitive firms in the domestic market in local currency.

- Lifetime utility of the household is given by

$$\max E_0 \sum_{t=0}^{\infty} \beta^t U(\acute{C}_t \; L_t)$$

where C_t^i and L_t^i aggregate consumption and labor supply.

- Period utility takes the following functional form:

$$U(C_t^i, L_t^i) = \frac{C_t^{i^{1-\sigma}}}{1-\sigma} - \phi_i \frac{L_t^{i^{1+\psi}}}{1+\psi}$$

- The consumption good C_t^i is a CES aggregate of tradable and non-tradable goods:

$$C_t^i = \left[b^{\frac{1}{\xi}} (C_{T,t}^i)^{\frac{\xi-1}{\xi}} + (1-b)^{\frac{1}{\xi}} (C_{N,t}^i)^{\frac{\xi-1}{\xi}} \right]^{\frac{\xi}{\xi-1}}$$

- Consumption of tradable goods $C_{T,t}^i$ is a CES aggregate of domestically and externally produced tradable goods:

$$C_{T,t}^i = \left[a^{\frac{1}{\eta}} (C_{H,t}^i)^{\frac{\eta-1}{\eta}} + (1-a)^{\frac{1}{\eta}} (C_{F,t}^i)^{\frac{\eta-1}{\eta}} \right]^{\frac{\eta}{\eta-1}}$$

- Differentiated, non-tradable goods are produced by monopolistically competitive producers:

$$C_{N,t}^i = \left[\int_0^1 C_{N,t}^i(j)^{\frac{\varepsilon-1}{\varepsilon}} dj \right]^{\frac{\varepsilon}{\varepsilon-1}}$$

- A typical household that derives labor income mainly from the non-tradable sector does not have access to financial markets and is modeled as a hand-to-mouth consumer with a budget constraint:

$$P_t C_t^N = W_{N,t} L_t^N + Profit_{N,t}$$

P_t denotes the price of the household's consumption basket, which includes tradable and non-tradable goods:

$$P_t = \left[b P_{T,t}^{1-\xi} + (1-b) P_{N,t}^{1-\xi} \right]^{\frac{1}{1-\xi}}$$

where

$$P_{T,t} = \left[a P_{H,t}^{1-\eta} + (1-a) P_{F,t}^{1-\eta} \right]^{\frac{1}{1-\eta}}$$

and

$$P_{N,t} = \left[\int_0^1 P_{N,t}(j)^{1-\varepsilon} dj \right]^{\frac{1}{1-\varepsilon}}$$

- A typical household in the tradable goods sector maximizes its lifetime utility subject to the budget constraint:

$$P_t C_t^T + B_t + e_t B_t^* + \frac{\varphi_B}{2} B_t^{*2} = W_{T,t} L_t^T + R_{t-1} B_{t-1} + e_t R_{t-1}^* B_{t-1}^*$$

- Tradable goods are produced competitively with a linear technology: $Y_{H,t} = A_{H,t} L_t^T$. Price of a home-produced tradable good follows the law of one price: $P_{H,t} = S_t P_{F,t}$, where S_t is the terms of trade.

- Monopolistically competitive non-tradable good producer j produces with a linear technology: $Y_{N,t}(j) = A_{N,t} L_t^N(j)$.

- Calvo pricing in non-tradables sector: only a fraction $1 - \theta$ of firms in this sector adjust their price in this sector, while the remaining firms keep the price from the previous period. Re-optimizing firms set their price to maximize the discounted sum of future profits:

$$\max_{P_{N,t}(j)} E_t \sum_{s=0}^{\infty} \left\{ (\beta\theta)^s \left(\frac{C_{t+s}^N}{P_{t+s}} \right)^{-\sigma} [P_{N,t}(j) - MC_{N,t+s}] Y_{N,t+s}(j) \right\}$$

A novel feature of the model is that it permits the study of the distributional consequences of alternative monetary policy and exchange rate regimes. These can play a key role in the political economy dynamics within a country that is exposed to large external shocks. For instance, consider the case of a productivity shock to the tradables sector. This normally implies a change in the equilibrium real exchange rate. If the central bank has adopted a fixed exchange rate rule, then the adjustment must come through domestic inflation. This can affect credit-constrained households differently than households that have access to financial markets for intertemporal consumption smoothing. It can also differentially affect households whose main source of income is labor income from the tradable goods sector versus the non-tradable goods sector. These distributional effects will be briefly touched upon in the discussion below, but deserve more careful attention than they have received in most of the existing literature.

Monetary Policy Rules

The central bank has three options, which range from a fixed (nominal) exchange rate to inflation targeting with a floating exchange rate. In each case, the policy rule includes interest rate smoothing, which reflects the tendency of central banks to incorporate a high degree of persistence in their policy rates and avoid large discrete changes.

1. Set the nominal interest rate so that the central bank responds aggressively to the deviation of the exchange rate from its value in the previous period. This represents a high degree of exchange rate smoothing and this regime is, in effect, a fixed exchange rate regime.[2]

$$log \left(\frac{R_t}{R} \right) = \rho_R log \left(\frac{R_{t-1}}{R} \right) + (1 - \rho_R) \left[\phi_\pi log \left(\frac{\pi_t}{\pi} \right) + \phi_e log \left(\frac{e_t}{e_{t-1}} \right) \right]$$

where $\phi_\pi > 1$ (Taylor principle) and ϕ_e is chosen to be "very large." In the numerical exercise, we set $\phi_e = 10$, $\phi_\pi = 1.5$.

2. Set the nominal interest rate to target inflation; the central bank does not respond to the deviation of the nominal exchange rate from its value in the previous period. This is, in effect, an inflation targeting regime.

$$log\left(\frac{R_t}{R}\right) = \rho_R log\left(\frac{R_{t-1}}{R}\right) + (1 - \rho_R)\phi_\pi log\left(\frac{\pi_t}{\pi}\right)$$

where $\phi_\pi > 1$ (Taylor principle), $\phi_e = 0$, $\phi_\pi = 1.5$.

3. Follow a mix of the two by changing the weights on nominal exchange rate changes and inflation in the policy rule.

The policy rule is thus set up in a way that allows intermediate policy options, wherein the central bank manages the exchange rate to varying degrees (essentially by changing the weights on inflation and nominal exchange rate changes in the policy rule). The model can, in principle, be adapted to study other types of regimes, such as real exchange rate targeting. The policy rules could also be extended in further work to capture flexible inflation targeting, wherein the central bank takes account of the output gap (the deviation of actual from potential output) in choosing its policy settings.

Shocks and Calibration

The experiments conducted using this model examine the effects of four main types of shocks that are relevant for developing economies:

1. Productivity shocks, tradable goods:

$$log\left(\frac{A_{H,t}}{A_H}\right) = \rho_a^H log\left(\frac{A_{H,t-1}}{A_H}\right) + \sigma_a^H \epsilon_t^H, \quad \epsilon_t^H \sim N(0,1)$$

2. Productivity shocks, non-tradable goods:

$$log\left(\frac{A_{N,t}}{A_N}\right) = \rho_a^N log\left(\frac{A_{N,t-1}}{A_N}\right) + \sigma_a^N \epsilon_t^N, \quad \epsilon_t^N \sim N(0,1)$$

3. Terms-of-trade shocks:

$$log\left(\frac{S_t}{S}\right) = \rho_s log\left(\frac{S_{t-1}}{S}\right) + \sigma^s \epsilon_t^s, \quad \epsilon_t^s \sim N(0,1)$$

4. Foreign interest rate shocks:

$$log\left(\frac{R_t^*}{R^*}\right) = \rho_R log\left(\frac{R_{t-1}^*}{R^*}\right) + \sigma^R \epsilon_t^R, \quad \epsilon_t^R \sim N(0,1)$$

Based on the analysis in the previous sections, terms-of-trade shocks are a key driver of macroeconomic fluctuations in ECOWAS countries. Productivity shocks also play a key role in both advanced and developing economies. For small open economies, it makes a big difference whether these shocks emanate in the traded or non-traded goods sector, so we model the shocks to the two sectors separately. Foreign interest rate shocks can have important implications for capital flows to developing economies, which, of course, matters greatly for economies with current account deficits. However, the low level of integration of ECOWAS economies into global financial markets implies that gross capital inflows and outflows are relatively modest.

Calibrating such models in the context of developing economies is a challenge. Both macro and micro studies of developing economies, from which such parameters can be taken, tend to be quite limited. Moreover, it proved difficult to get sufficient data for ECOWAS economies to conduct a full-scale Bayesian estimation of the key model parameters. Hence, the approach taken below is to draw upon the existing literature to the extent possible in identifying relevant parameter values and then conducting robustness tests using different values of parameters for which such information was sparse. This aspect of the analysis can be improved upon in the future as more data becomes available, but it may still be unrealistic to estimate country-specific parameters for ECOWAS economies.

Table C-1 lists the key parameters of the model, the values assigned to them in the baseline simulations, and the sources that those values are based on.

Results

This subsection summarizes the dynamics of key variables in the model in response to various shocks, and outlines welfare calculations in response to these shocks.

Figure C-1 shows the dynamics of overall inflation in response to different shocks under the two polar regimes—fixed exchange rate and inflation targeting with a flexible exchange rate. Figure C-2 shows the corresponding responses of output. In the case of productivity and terms-of-trade shocks, the level of inflation usually responds to these shocks in a similar way under either regime. But inflation tends to be more volatile under a fixed exchange rate regime.

In the case of a positive foreign interest rate shock, the pass-through of nominal exchange depreciation to domestic prices leads to a rise in inflation, along with a rise in domestic output, under an IT regime. The impact effect of the shock actually pushes down inflation in the fixed exchange rate regime. It can be seen from the responses of other variables that the differential inflation response under the two regimes is the result of a contraction in activity in the non-tradables sector, which is the result of the central bank increasing the domestic policy interest rate in order to keep the exchange rate stable.

One implication of this discussion is that it is important to evaluate alternative regimes not just in terms of how inflation is affected but also in terms of how output and employment are affected. In other words, one needs to look explicitly at the overall welfare consequences under alternative scenarios. A second issue is that it is not just the impact effects but also the medium- and long-run responses of the variables that could be quite different under alternative regimes. In the case of the foreign interest rate shock, an inflation targeting central bank would tighten monetary policy after the impact effect feeds through to domestic prices. But this tightening could have slightly larger adverse effects on output, consumption, and employment relative to those under a fixed exchange rate regime.

Next, we discuss the welfare implications of different monetary and exchange rate regimes. Table C-2 reports welfare comparisons between an inflation targeting regime with a floating nominal exchange rate versus a fixed exchange rate regime. A positive number shows the gain in welfare, expressed as a percent of lifetime consumption, under the former regime relative to the latter. The table shows welfare calculations for representative households in the traded and non-traded goods sectors and also an aggregate welfare calculation, which weights households in each sector by their weight in the population (the relevant parameter, l, is set at 0.6, meaning that 60 percent of households derive their income from the traded goods sector).

The key result is that, in response to different sources of shocks, there are significant welfare gains with flexible rather than fixed exchange rates. In the face of terms-of-trade shocks, which are most relevant for small commodity-exporting economies, the welfare gain from the former regime

TABLE C-1. **Parameterization of the Baseline DSGE Model: Key Model Parameters**

Parameter	Definition	Value	Source
β	Discount factor	0.99	Risk free rate of 4 percent
σ	Risk aversion	2	Standard in the literature— the cycle is the trend
λ	Share of households in the tradable-good sector	0.6	
a	Weight on domestically produced tradable goods in the total tradable goods basket	0.7	Obstfeld and Rogoff (2001)
b	Weight on tradable goods in the total consumption basket	0.295	Share of agriculture and manufacturing in Nigerian GDP (value added), 2017, WDI
ε	Elasticity of substitution between non-tradable varieties	11	Clarida, Gali, and Gertler (1999)
η	Elasticity of substitution between home and foreign produced tradable goods	2	Obstfeld and Rogoff (2005, 2007)
ξ	Elasticity of substitution between tradable and non-tradable goods in the consumption basket	1.36	Ostry and Reinhart (1992)
ψ	Inverse of Frisch elasticity of labor supply	3	Dagher (2012), standard value, Ghana

Parameter	Definition	Value	Source
ψ_b	Interest rate elasticity of debt	0.0007	Included for technical reasons
θ	Probability of not resetting price in a given quarter	0.75	To yield an average duration of a price of one year
ρ	Interest rate smoothing parameter	0.75	Clarida, Gali, and Gertler (1999)
ϕ_π	Response to the deviation of inflation from the steady state	1.5	Clarida, Gali, and Gertler (1999)
ϕ_y	Response to output gap	0.125	Prasad and Zhang (2015)
ϕ_e	Response to nominal exchange rate depreciation	0 or 10	0 for flexible inflation targeting; 10 for fixed exchange rate regime
ρ_h, σ_h	Persistence and standard deviation of tradable good productivity	0.9, 0.020	Prasad and Zhang (2015)
ρ_n, σ_n	Persistence and standard deviation of non-tradable good productivity	0.9, 0.015	Prasad and Zhang (2015)
ρ_{tot}, σ_{tot}	Persistence and standard deviation of terms of trade shocks	0.52, 0.08	Schmitt-Grohe and Uribe (2018)
ρ_{R^*}, σ_{R^*}	Persistence and standard deviation of foreign interest rate shocks	0.46, 0.012	Devereux, Lane, and Xu (2006)

FIGURE c-1. Response of Inflation to Different Shocks
Under Fixed and Floating Exchange Rates

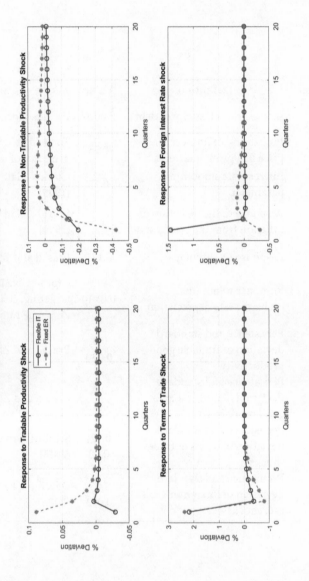

FIGURE C-2. **Response of Output to Different Shocks
Under Fixed and Floating Exchange Rates**

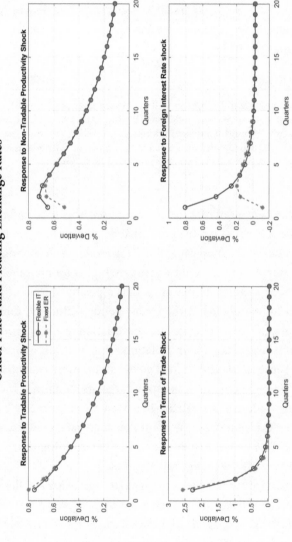

TABLE C-2. **Welfare Comparisons: Inflation Targeting with Floating Exchange Rate Relative to Fixed Exchange Rate**

Shock to:	Households in tradables sector	Households in non-tradables sector	Aggregate
Tradables productivity	0.003	0.004	0.003
Non-tradables productivity	0.036	0.059	0.045
Terms of trade	0.045	0.079	0.059
Foreign interest rate	−0.011	−0.009	−0.010

Notes: Numbers above are differences in welfare, expressed as percent of lifetime consumption, in a flexible exchange rate regime with inflation targeting relative to the benchmark, which is a fixed exchange rate regime. A positive number indicates higher welfare in the alternative regime compared to the benchmark. The two regimes are defined in the context of the model as follows: IT with flexible exchange rate: $\phi_\pi = 1.5$, $\phi_e = 0$; fixed exchange rate: $\phi_\pi = 1.5$, $\phi_e = 10$.

is about 0.6 percent of lifetime consumption. This is consistent with an extensive literature making the point that flexible exchange rates provide important shock absorption capabilities for small open economies.[3]

More important, the welfare gains are higher for households in the non-traded goods sector. The reason is that a positive terms-of-trade shock is beneficial to households in the traded goods sector but, under a fixed exchange rate, the real exchange rate appreciation resulting from such a shock results in a larger increase in inflation. This hurts all households but particularly those in the non-traded goods sector. Consequently, a flexible exchange rate regime with an inflation target as a nominal anchor results in even larger welfare gains, relative to a fixed exchange rate, for households in this sector. This reinforces the point that aggregate, as well as distributional effects, need to be taken into account in determining the welfare implications of alternative exchange rate regimes.

The gains from a flexible exchange rate regime are smaller in response to other types of shocks. Moreover, in the case of foreign interest rate shocks, a fixed exchange rate yields higher welfare. But it should be noted that this is because the rise in inflation associated with this shock elicits a stronger monetary policy response from the central bank, which drives down output and employment. Under a fixed exchange rate regime, the central bank is more tolerant of inflation in response to this source of shocks.

One of key parameters in the model is the elasticity of substitution between tradable and non-tradable goods. For advanced countries, this parameter is typically estimated as being less than one. This is potentially because

TABLE C-3. **Welfare Comparisons with Alternative Elasticity of Substitution between Tradables and Non-Tradables**

Shock to:	Households in tradables sector	Households in non-tradables sector	Aggregate
Tradables productivity	0.002	0.004	0.003
Non-tradables productivity	0.027	0.051	0.037
Terms of trade	0.065	0.131	0.091
Foreign interest rate	−0.061	−0.106	−0.079

Notes: Numbers above are differences in welfare, expressed as percent of lifetime consumption, in a flexible exchange rate regime with inflation targeting relative to the benchmark, which is a fixed exchange rate regime. A positive number indicates higher welfare in the alternative regime compared to the benchmark. The two regimes are defined in the context of the model as follows: IT with flexible exchange rate: $\phi_\pi = 1.5$, $\phi_e = 0$; fixed exchange rate: $\phi_\pi = 1.5$, $\phi_e = 10$.

durables account for a sizable portion of traded goods, while nondurables are mainly non-traded goods. The same elasticity for African countries is estimated to be in the region 1.279–1.441. The results above use the average value from such studies of $\xi = 1.36$. Robustness tests using higher and lower values of this parameter (from 1.0 to 1.5) showed that the main conclusions are preserved. For instance, table C-3 shows the welfare calculations using a value of $\xi = 1.5$. The results are qualitatively similar. One important difference is that, in response to terms-of-trade shocks, the welfare gains from an inflation targeting regime with a floating exchange rate are even higher relative to a fixed exchange rate regime.

Mechanisms

This section provides an overview of the mechanisms for the shock response results reported in the main part of the paper. The impulse responses for selected variables whose dynamics are discussed below and more detailed analysis can be found in Prasad (2019).

1. *Positive productivity shock in tradable goods sector*
   - A positive tradable productivity shock leads to an increase in the relative price of non-tradable goods. This leads to real exchange rate appreciation (since RER is determined by the relative price of non-tradable goods). RER impulse responses (not shown here) confirm this.
   - Output, consumption (aggregate, tradable, non-tradable), and tradable employment rise initially, but the real appreciation leads to

lower level of output and tradable employment in later response horizons.

- Non-tradable employment rises upon impact but shrinks in subsequent periods due to higher marginal cost. The increase in wages in the tradable sector will also lead to higher wages in the non-tradable sector, and hence higher marginal cost.

- Tradable inflation falls, while non-tradable inflation rises. The effect on aggregate inflation depends on the monetary policy regime. Inflation falls in a flexible inflation targeting regime, while it rises in a fixed exchange rate regime.

- The positive productivity shock in the tradable sector results in higher inflation under a fixed exchange rate regime, since the nominal rate does not absorb the shock and monetary policy is committed to maintaining the nominal exchange rate at a fixed level. In a flexible inflation targeting regime, inflation falls due to the monetary policy response.

2. *Positive productivity shock in non-tradable goods sector*
   - A positive productivity shock in the non-tradable sector leads to a fall in the relative price of non-tradable goods and, hence, leads to a real depreciation.

   - Aggregate output rises despite the decline in employment in both traded and non-traded sectors. This is the effect of higher productivity in the non-tradable sector. Consumption, aggregate as well as sectoral, rises.

   - Inflation: the positive shock in the non-tradable sector will decrease inflation in the non-tradable sector while higher wages (and hence higher marginal cost) lead to higher inflation in the tradable sector. On the aggregate, inflation falls in both the fixed exchange rate and flexible inflation targeting regimes. However, the fall inflation is mitigated in the case of flexible inflation targeting regime, since the nominal exchange rate plays the role of a shock absorber.

3. *Positive terms-of-trade shock*
   - Aggregate output, tradable employment, and non-tradable employment increase.

   - A positive terms-of-trade shock creates pressure on the domestic currency to appreciate.

- Monetary policy aimed at maintaining the exchange rate regime will magnify the effect of a terms-of-trade shock on output (Broda and Tille (2003)). In a fixed exchange rate regime, the central bank will have to increase money supply to cancel out the pressure on the currency to appreciate. This means that the increase in output and employment will be higher in a fixed exchange rate regime than flexible inflation targeting regime. (This is clear from the impulse responses for non-tradable employment and aggregate output.)

- Aggregate, tradable, and non-tradable inflation all rise upon impact but fall soon thereafter. In a fixed exchange rate regime, this is because of the expansionary monetary policy that strives to maintain the exchange rate. In a flexible exchange rate regime, this is due to the increase in the price of home-produced traded goods.

4. *Positive shock to foreign interest rate*
   - Output rises in a flexible inflation targeting regime but falls in a fixed exchange rate regime. In the latter regime, the central bank must increase the domestic interest rate to remove the pressure on the currency to depreciate. This will be contractionary.

   - The contractionary monetary policy implemented with the aim of maintaining the fixed exchange rate will also result in a decrease in the rate of inflation. In a flexible inflation targeting regime, the central bank does not respond to changes in the nominal exchange rate. Hence the currency depreciation will pass through to domestic prices and will result in higher inflation. Therefore, the response of inflation to foreign interest rate shocks depends critically on the exchange rate regime.

   - An inflation-targeting central bank will respond by raising interest rates (to fight off the inflation from the passthrough), which will decrease output and employment more in the long run. (This long-run effect is mitigated in a fixed exchange rate regime, as the currency depreciation will be limited or absent.) So, while a fixed exchange rate regime implies a contractionary monetary policy in the short run, flexible inflation targeting implies a contractionary monetary policy in the long run. In the baseline parametrization, the latter effect dominates the former and welfare effects are negative.

SUMMARY

The main conclusion drawn from the analysis above is that for a developing economy characterized by credit constraints, nominal price rigidities, and vulnerability to terms of trade and other external shocks, an inflation targeting regime with a floating nominal exchange rate delivers superior welfare outcomes relative to a fixed exchange rate that implies lack of autonomy for domestic monetary policy. This result should be seen as providing guidance rather than as a definitive conclusion, since it is based on a particular model and is not necessarily "fitted" to the specific circumstances or data of any particular ECOWAS country. Nevertheless, the conclusion is fairly robust no matter what the source of external shocks and the different values of key model parameters.

Another option for a nominal anchor under a floating exchange rate would be the targeting of a region-wide monetary aggregate. This approach certainly has appeal, given the lack of well-integrated financial markets and lack of clarity about the monetary transmission mechanism—in particular, about how short-term policy rates influence inflation and economic activity. But these same considerations make monetary targeting even more challenging, both in terms of managing monetary policy and in maintaining its credibility. In addition, as with inflation and economic activity, devising ECOWAS-wide measures of relevant monetary aggregates poses substantial challenges in view of substantial differences in data concepts and quality across the zone.

An inflation target would serve as a better nominal anchor when the new monetary authority for the currency zone is striving to build credibility and manage monetary policy in an uncertain environment in which the relationship between monetary aggregates and inflation/output at the ECOWAS level is not well determined and could be particularly unstable during the transition process. Thus, a better option would be to use the behavior of monetary aggregates to help fine-tune the use of a battery of monetary policy instruments that are already used by different countries in the region (short-term policy rates, reserve requirements, open market operations) in achieving an inflation target.

As noted by Mishkin (2000) in the context of emerging market economies, "In contrast to monetary targeting . . . inflation targeting has the advantage that a stable relationship between money and inflation is not critical to its success; the strategy does not depend on such a relationship but instead uses all available information to determine the best settings for the instruments of monetary policy. Inflation targeting also has the key advantage that it is easily understood by the public and is thus highly transparent."

While it might be a better alternative than monetary targeting, given the circumstances in ECOWAS, inflation targeting poses its own challenges in terms of data and information requirements. Thus, the issues raised in chapter 7 of this book about the technical and institutional underpinnings needed for effective monetary policy are crucial ones for any nominal anchor to be implemented successfully.

APPENDIX D

Details on Construction of Data for Analytical Exercises

The vector autoregression (VAR) analysis in the report is based on nonstructural or reduced-form panel vector autoregressions (PVAR) proposed by Holtz-Eakin and others (1988). These statistical models are useful for dealing with large panels of time series data; see Canova and Ciccarelli (2013), Pesaran and others (2004), Chudik and Pesaran (2011), and Pesaran (2015). They impose specific types of restrictions on the VAR parameters to allow larger VAR models to be estimated.

Large panels of variables often arise in studies of different countries or regions, but also when dealing with sectors, firms, plants, or households. For example, we may denote the tth observation for the ith variable of country n by y_{int}, where $i = 1, \ldots, M$ and $n = 1, \ldots, N$. Thus, the size of the dataset is $K = M \cdot N$. In this case, we have $M = 3$ and $N = 6$. Let

$$y_{nt} = (y_{1nt}, \ldots, y_{Mnt})'$$

be an M-dimensional vector and denote by $Y_{n,t-1}$ and Y_{t-1} vectors of lags of y_{nt} and all variables in the panel, respectively. Then the model for y_{nt} has the general form

$$y_{nt} = v_n + A_n Y_{t-1} + u_{nt}, \tag{1}$$

with fully general error covariance matrix Σu for the system of all N units, where Σu is the covariance matrix of $'$ $u_t = (u_{1t}, ..., u_{Nt})$. In the panel VAR model represented in equation 1, the data vector, y_{nt}, is {TOT, INF, GDP} where TOT stands for the terms of trade (levels or changes), INF is the inflation rate based on consumer prices, and GDP is real GDP growth.

Table D-1 presents the macroeconomic variables used in the PVAR model and provides a detailed description of the data. The data series, which are all annual, are collected from the International Financial Statistics (IFS), World Development Indicators (WDI), and Federal Reserve Economic Data (FRED). The full set of data required for the analysis presented in the report were available for only six of the fifteen ECOWAS countries: Côte d'Ivoire, Ghana, Nigeria, Sierra Leone, the Gambia, and Togo. Table D-2 provides summary statistics for the dataset.

Table D-3 shows some statistical results relevant for the choice of lag length in the estimated model. Table D-4 shows forecast error variance decompositions from three-variable VARs with GDP growth, inflation, and changes in the terms of trade. These variance decompositions show that shocks to changes in the terms of trade make only a modest contribution to GDP growth and inflation fluctuations in the non-WAEMU countries in the sample.

Table D-5 provides details on the dataset and the construction of variables for the estimation of Taylor rules reported in chapter 6.

TABLE D-1. Data Description

Nature of the Shocks	Shocks	Proxies and Descriptions	Sources
Domestic Shocks	Output Growth	Real GDP growth (annual %) Growth (YoY) of real GDP	WB-WDI
	Inflation	Inflation, consumer prices (annual %) Growth (YoY) of consumer price index (CPI, 2010 = 100)	WB-WDI
	Terms of Trade	Terms of trade (ToT) index for goods The ratio between export price index and import price index (2010 = 100)	IMF-IFS
External Shocks	World Interest Rate	U.S. short-term interest rates (%) A volume-weighted median of overnight federal funds transactions reported in the FR 2420 Report of Selected Money Market Rates (effective federal funds rate)	FRED
	Uncertainty in Global Financial Markets	VIX (index) The stock market's expectation of volatility implied by S&P 500 index options.	FRED
	World Output Growth	World GDP growth (annual %) Real growth (YoY) of global GDP	WB-WDI

Notes: WB-WDI = World Development Indicators, World Bank; IMF-IFS = International Financial Statistics, International Monetary Fund; and FRED = Federal Reserve Economic Data.

TABLE D-2. **Summary Statistics**

Variables	Mean	S.D.	Min	Max	N
Domestic Indicators					
GDP growth (percent)	3.6	5.7	−20.6	26.4	294
Inflation, CPI (percent)	13.4	17.6	−5.4	122.9	256
External Indicators					
Merchandise terms of trade (index)	96.0	24.9	51.0	216.3	84
Merchandise terms of trade (changes, in %)	0.1	13.8	−50.0	33.5	78
World GDP growth (percent)	3.2	1.5	−1.7	6.6	294
U.S. short-term interest rates (percent)	5.3	4.0	0.1	18.9	294
VIX (index)	19.3	5.9	11.1	32.6	168

Notes: The table presents the summary statistics for the six countries considered in the regression analysis.

TABLE D-3. Lag-Order Selection Criteria

Lag	CD	J	J p-value	MBIC	MAIC	MQIC
1	0.81	22.82	0.69	−80.55	−31.18	−49.67
2	0.87	21.15	0.27	−47.76	−14.85	−27.18
3	0.80	7.95	0.54	−26.51	−10.05	−16.22

Notes: The table presents the computed information criteria for panel VAR models with three variables including GDP growth, CPI inflation, and terms-of-trade changes. The sample covers six countries (Nigeria, Ghana, Côte d'Ivoire, Togo, Sierra Leone, and The Gambia) over the period 2009–2016, yielding forty-six observations. The lag length of the VAR model, determined using the moment model selection criteria (MMSC) developed by Andrews and Lu (2001), is one. Similar to maximum likelihood-based information criteria AIC, BIC, and HQIC, the model that minimizes the MMSC-Bayesian information criterion (MBIC), MMSC-Akaike information criterion (MAIC), or MMSC-Hannan and Quinn information criterion (MQIC) is the preferred model.

TABLE D-4. Variance Decompositions: VARs with GDP Growth, Inflation, Terms-of-Trade Changes

A. ECOWAS

Forecast horizon	GDP growth: sources of fluctutation			CPI Inflation: Sources of Fluctuation		
	GDP growth	CPI inflation	Terms of Trade	GDP growth	CPI inflation	Terms of Trade
0	0.00	0.00	0.00	0.00	0.00	0.00
1	1.00	0.00	0.00	0.06	0.94	0.00
2	0.99	0.01	0.00	0.29	0.71	0.00
3	0.98	0.02	0.00	0.35	0.64	0.00
4	0.98	0.02	0.00	0.38	0.62	0.00
5	0.98	0.02	0.00	0.39	0.61	0.00
6	0.98	0.02	0.00	0.39	0.61	0.00
7	0.98	0.02	0.00	0.39	0.61	0.00
8	0.98	0.02	0.00	0.39	0.61	0.00
9	0.98	0.02	0.00	0.39	0.61	0.00
10	0.98	0.02	0.00	0.39	0.61	0.00

B. WAEMU

Forecast horizon	GDP growth: sources of fluctutation			CPI Inflation: Sources of Fluctuation		
	GDP growth	CPI inflation	Terms of Trade	GDP growth	CPI inflation	Terms of Trade
0	0.00	0.00	0.00	0.00	0.00	0.00
1	1.00	0.00	0.00	0.00	1.00	0.00
2	1.00	0.00	0.00	0.01	0.92	0.07
3	0.99	0.00	0.01	0.01	0.92	0.07
4	0.99	0.00	0.01	0.01	0.92	0.07
5	0.99	0.00	0.01	0.01	0.92	0.07
6	0.99	0.00	0.01	0.01	0.92	0.07
7	0.99	0.00	0.01	0.01	0.92	0.07
8	0.99	0.00	0.01	0.01	0.92	0.07
9	0.99	0.00	0.01	0.01	0.92	0.07
10	0.99	0.00	0.01	0.01	0.92	0.07

c. Non-WAEMU (Ghana, Nigeria, The Gambia)MU

Forecast horizon	GDP growth: sources of fluctutation			CPI Inflation: Sources of Fluctuation		
	GDP growth	CPI inflation	Terms of Trade	GDP growth	CPI inflation	Terms of Trade
0	0.00	0.00	0.00	0.00	0.00	0.00
1	1.00	0.00	0.00	0.14	0.86	0.00
2	0.81	0.08	0.11	0.28	0.67	0.06
3	0.81	0.08	0.11	0.33	0.59	0.08
4	0.79	0.09	0.12	0.35	0.56	0.09
5	0.79	0.09	0.12	0.36	0.54	0.09
6	0.79	0.09	0.12	0.36	0.54	0.10
7	0.79	0.09	0.12	0.37	0.54	0.10
8	0.79	0.09	0.12	0.37	0.53	0.10
9	0.79	0.09	0.12	0.37	0.53	0.10
10	0.79	0.09	0.12	0.37	0.53	0.10

Notes: This table presents forecast error variance decompositions from three-variable VARs, with GDP growth, inflation, and terms-of-trade changes. The numbers shown are shares of total forecast error variance of relevant variables at different forecast horizons attributable to shocks to different variables in the model.

TABLE D-5. **Variables and Descriptions**

Variable	Country	Source	Note
Annual CPI	ECOWAS WAEMU Ghana Nigeria	World Economic Outlook (April 2019)	Series: inflation, average consumer prices. Weighted-average CPI for ECOWAS and WAEMU, weighted by 2018 nominal GDP in U.S. dollar terms.
Output level (2000 = 100)	ECOWAS WAEMU Ghana Nigeria	World Economic Outlook (April 2019)	Series: Gross domestic product, current prices, USD, in billions. (1) All member states' output levels are set as 100 in 2018. Weights are calculated using 2018 nominal GDP for the two blocs. (2) Series are then reset as 100 in 2000.
Output growth	ECOWAS WAEMU Ghana Nigeria	Calculation	Percentage change in output level.
Output gap (HP filter, λ = 100, in natural log)	ECOWAS WAEMU Ghana Nigeria	Calculation	Convert to natural log, then use a HP filter (λ = 100). Since HP filters are sensitive to values at the two ends, which may cause serious selection biases, the HP trend is estimated using data from 1990 to 2018 instead of from 2000 to 2018.
Output gap (linear time trend, in natural log)	ECOWAS WAEMU Ghana Nigeria	Calculation	Convert to natural log, then use a linear trend. To avoid structural changes in past data, unlike in the HP filter method, past data (before 2000) are not used here.

Year-end policy rates	WAEMU	International Financial Statistics, Bank of Ghana	Only data from 2001 to 2018 are available.
	Ghana		Data from Bank of Ghana.
	Nigeria		00-06: Discount rate; 07-18: Policy rate.
	ECOWAS	Calculation	Weighted by 2018 nominal GDP in U.S. dollar terms.
Period-average exchange rates	WAEMU	International Financial Statistics	Period-average exchange rates against USD.
	Ghana		
	Nigeria		
	ECOWAS	Calculation	Weighted by 2018 nominal GDP in U.S. dollar terms. Weights are assigned to the powers of components.

NOTES

CHAPTER 1

1. We use the terms "monetary union" and "currency union" interchangeably in this book. A common currency implies that each country in the union forsakes independent monetary policy.

2. Data on per capita GDP in constant prices, PPP adjusted to 2011 international dollars, are from the IMF October 2018 WEO database.

3. The WAEMU countries are Benin, Burkina Faso, Côte d'Ivoire, Guinea-Bissau, Mali, Niger, Senegal, and Togo. WAEMU was formed in 1994, building upon the West African Monetary Union, which was created in 1973. The CFA franc zone also includes six other countries that comprise the Central African Economic and Monetary Union (CAEMU): Cameroon, Central African Republic, Chad, Republic of Congo, Equatorial Guinea, and Gabon.

4. Daude and others (2014) document the prevalence of this "leaning against the wind" exchange rate intervention in emerging economies. These authors also show that such a policy does mitigate real exchange rate volatility.

CHAPTER 2

1. This is the classic model of dynamically consistent monetary policy, due to Barro and Gordon (1983). Also Rogoff (1985) and Calvo and Vegh (1994).

2. Going back to the original proponent of floating exchange rates: Friedman (1953).

3. One piece of evidence is that nominal changes in the exchange rate are seen to

cause real changes in the exchange rate. For example, Bahmani-Oskooee, Hegerty, and Kutan (2008).

4. For a survey of the criticisms leveled against this literature, see Baldwin (2006). Also see Nitsch (2002). Some of these criticisms are addressed in Rose and van Wincoop (2001), Persson (2001), Frankel (2010), and Rose (2017).

5. There are other channels through which currency depreciations, rather than stimulating net exports and helping to revive growth, can be contractionary (for example, Frankel (2005)). This particularly applies to a country that has a lot of debt denominated in foreign currency. Currency mismatch plus devaluation results in a negative balance sheet effect, which is one explanation for the observed "fear of floating" (Calvo and Reinhart (2002)). The shock absorption properties of nominal exchange rates have also been questioned by the Dominant Currency Pricing (DCP) literature. Papers in this literature, such as Gopinath and others (2020), argue that a country whose exports are mostly priced in a dominant currency, such as the U.S. dollar, might see only a modest benefit from a currency depreciation.

6. Other papers with similar findings include Broda (2004), Edwards and Levy-Yeyati (2005), Rafiq (2011), and Berg, Goncalves, and Portillo (2018).

7. Examples include Ghosh, Gulde, and Wolf (2000), Sturzenegger and Levy-Yeyati (2001, 2003), Reinhart and Rogoff (2004), Tavlas, Dellas, and Stockman (2008), and Klein and Shambaugh (2012).

8. The low correspondence across different analysts' classifications of countries by exchange rate regime has been documented by Bénassy-Quéré, Coeuré, and Mignon (2004), Frankel (2003), Klein and Shambaugh (2013), and Rose (2011). One reason for differences in classification outcomes is differences in methodology. A more fundamental problem is that many countries, in fact, do not typically follow any single regime for longer than a year or so without changing parameters, if not changing regimes altogether.

9. Obstfeld and Rogoff (1995) and Klein and Marion (1997) document that most declared pegs do not last very long [absent an institutional elimination of the possibility of devaluation; for example, through a currency union].

10. Cossé and others (1996) and Devarajan and Hinkle (1994).

11. For a useful overview of the economic and political tensions that have dogged the euro zone since its inception, and how those tensions affected some of the weaker countries in the zone, see Mody (2018).

12. Debrun, Masson, and Pattillo (2005).

13. Frankel and Rose (2002) find that a currency union has a strong positive effect on trade flows among the members of the union and suggest that much of this gain comes from the elimination of exchange rate risk. They also find that, rather than diverting trade, members of a currency union increase their trade even with other countries outside the union.

14. The ASEAN countries are Brunei, Cambodia, Indonesia, Laos, Malaysia, Myanmar, Philippines, Singapore, Thailand, and Vietnam.

15. Goswami and Sharma (2011) discuss the development of local debt markets in Asia.

16. See Gilbert, Scollay, and Bora (2001), Elliott and Ikomoto (2004), Jugurnath, Stewart, and Brooks (2007), Bun, Klaassen, and Tan (2009), Kitwiwattanachai,

Nelson, and Reed (2010), Itakura (2014), Yang and Martinez-Zarzoso (2014), Ji and others (2018), Maliszewska, Olekseyuk, and Osorio-Rodarte (2018).

17. Coulibaly (2009) reports one additional potential benefit. He finds that membership in a currency union reduces vulnerability to currency crises.

18. See Mundell (1961), McKinnon (1963), and Kenen (1969) for the classical OCA criteria.

19. Tavlas (2008).

CHAPTER 3

1. See IMF WAEMU Staff Report, www.imf.org/en/Publications/CR/Issues/2019/03/29/West-African-Economic-and-Monetary-Union-WAEMU-Staff-Report-on-Common-Policies-for-Member-46723.

2. A significant portion of this decline in the U.S. share is accounted for by a fall in the share of Nigeria's exports to the United States (and a concomitant rise in Nigeria's exports, mainly of oil, to India). Excluding Nigeria (see table 3-2), the overall share of intra-ECOWAS trade in the total trade of the zone's member countries is 12 percent (the corresponding share of exports is 16 percent).

3. There are some indications of a significant amount of informal cross-border trade in Africa that is not reflected in official trade statistics. However, as noted in a recent AfDB report, even taking account of such informal trade would leave the degree of intra-African trade well below intra-regional trade in other parts of the world. For instance, the report notes that intra-regional trade in Europe and Asia, as a share of these regions' total trade, exceeds 65 percent and 40 percent, respectively.

4. Part of this decline is no doubt because of weak demand growth in the eurozone in the aftermath of the debt crisis. It is interesting to note from table 3-3 that the export shares of the United States and Nigeria also fell over this period, while the shares accounted for by other WEAMU countries and by India increased significantly.

5. This section draws extensively on Vera Songwe (2019) "Intra-African Trade: A Path to Economic Diversification and Inclusion," Brookings Institution. https://www.brookings.edu/research/intra-african-trade-a-path-to-economic-diversification-and-inclusion/

6. See "African Trade Report 2018," African Export-Import Bank, July 2018, www.tralac.org/documents/news/2042-african-trade-report-2018-afreximbank/file.html.

7. See "Assessment of AfCFTA Modalities," United Nations Economic Commission for Africa, November 2018, www.uneca.org/sites/default/files/Publication Files/brief_assessment_of_afcfta_modalities_eng_nov18.pdf.

8. See "Economic Development in Africa: 2019 Report," United Nations Conference on Trade and Development, June 2019, https://unctad.org/en/Publications Library/aldcafrica2019_en.pdf.

9. See "The Diversification Toolkit: Export Diversification and Quality Databases," International Monetary Fund, December 2019, www.imf.org/external/np/res/dfidimf/diversification.htm.

10. See "Assessment of AfCFTA Modalities," United Nations Economic Com-

mission for Africa, November 2018, www.uneca.org/sites/default/files/Publication Files/brief_assessment_of_afcfta_modalities_eng_nov18.pdf.

CHAPTER 4

1. High levels of foreign currency–denominated external debt have been identified as a proximate determinant of a number of previous balance-of-payment crises in emerging markets. Even if these are debt obligations of private corporations, they can have systemic macroeconomic consequences through balance sheet effects precipitated by currency mismatches (depreciation of the local currency increases the local currency value of foreign currency debt, which can create liquidity and solvency problems for corporations, especially those with mainly local currency revenues).

2. Since the IMF no longer reports reserves data for individual WAEMU countries, these country counts are based on WAEMU totals for reserves, external debt, and other relevant variables. Total reserves for WAEMU countries stood at USD 15.8 billion in 2019, according to the IMF. This would amount to roughly 41.9 percent of WAEMU external debt. Local currency-denominated debt held by foreign investors poses less of a risk than foreign currency–denominated external debt. It was not possible to get this breakdown, but it seems a reasonable assumption that most of the external debt of ECOWAS countries is foreign currency debt as is typically the case for developing economies.

3. For more details about the construction and interpretation of the indexes, see IMF (2014).

4. The analysis in this section is based largely on work done by Tsenguunjav Byambasuren.

5. Detailed results are reported in Prasad (2019). While many of the macroeconomic data are available for more countries and over a longer period, consistent data on terms of trade proved to be the binding constraint.

6. Larger VARs that could help analyze these channels could not be estimated because of the lack of data, especially the limited time series dimension of the sample.

7. See Prasad (2019) for variance decompositions from VARs that use changes rather than levels of the terms of trade.

8. Mendoza (1995) shows that terms-of-trade shocks account for nearly half of GDP variability across a broad sample of countries, with the effects being particularly large for developing economies. Hoffmaister and Roldos (2001), using vector autoregression techniques, confirm this result for selected emerging market economies. Deaton and Miller (1996) find that external shocks, especially terms-of-trade shocks, have a large influence on fluctuations of output and the real exchange rate in CFA franc countries, especially relative to non-CFA franc countries in sub-Saharan Africa. Cashin, McDermott, and Pattillo (2004) conclude that terms-of-trade shocks, which they find to be large and highly persistent, are a key determinant of macroeconomic performance in sub-Saharan African economies.

9. The CDIS is based on data self-reported by countries to the IMF. This dataset, which captures the immediate sources of FDI stocks (rather than annual flows), has a number of well-known lacunae, and its coverage tends to be spotty for emerging

market and developing economies. A comparable database for portfolio flows, the IMF's Coordinated Portfolio Investment Survey, has even more sparse coverage for developing economies, which is not surprising, since many of these economies have underdeveloped equity markets and some of them also restrict access to foreign investors.

10. One study indicates that, as of 2014, non-concessional debt accounted for 20 percent of Senegal's external debt, up from 0 percent in 2008. In other words, Senegal is gaining increasing access to international capital markets, but this also raises its vulnerability to capital flow shocks. Its vulnerability is limited at this stage. See Mansoor, Issoufou, and Sembene (2018).

11. For instance, some countries exclude from the labor force discouraged workers and others who are not actively seeking employment, and do not consider such workers as unemployed.

12. See Prasad (2019) for data and more detailed analysis.

13. The WEF reports did not have data for Burkina Faso, Côte d'Ivoire, Guinea Bissau, Niger, and Togo.

CHAPTER 5

1. The 2018 IMF Staff Report on Nigeria notes the "ongoing convergence of exchange rate windows" and lists the "multitude of exchange rates" that remain, including: (1) the CBN official window, (2) retail/wholesale window, (3) Investors and Exporters Foreign Exchange (IFEX) window, and (4) rate at which CBN sells foreign exchange for invisibles transactions, Bureaux de Changes, and small and medium enterprises. In early 2019, the U.S. dollar was trading against the naira at a premium in the range of 17–18 percent in the parallel market (Bureaux de Changes rate) relative to the official central bank rate.

2. As of April 2019, 171 of the IMF's 192 members had accepted the obligations of Article VIII, Sections 2, 3, and 4.

3. For an overview of the theoretical issues and the extensive empirical evidence on this matter, see "Monetary Policy Frameworks in EMEs: Inflation Targeting, the Exchange Rate, and Financial Stability," Bank for International Settlements, June 2019. https://www.bis.org/publ/arpdf/ar2019e2.htm

4. For an exposition of the dominant currency paradigm, see Gopinath and others (2020).

5. For more details, see "China's Monetary Policy and the Bond Market," S&P Global Ratings, February 2019, www.spglobal.com/en/research-insights/articles/china-s-monetary-policy-and-the-bond-market, or IMF staff reports on China.

CHAPTER 6

1. The analysis in this chapter is based largely on work done by Yang Liu.

2. There is a growing literature in this area. Mohanty and Klau (2005) undertake such an exercise for emerging market economies, incorporating an exchange rate variable explicitly to account for these economies' desire for exchange rate stability. Goncalves (2015) uses VAR models to estimate Taylor rule parameters for some African countries. Other papers that have undertaken such exercises for African economies include Siri (2012) and Diop, Tillman, and Winker (2017).

3. The corresponding correlations for the period 2009–15 are slightly less negative at –0.22 and –0.39, respectively. The composite measures of GDP growth are based on GDP weights at either market exchange rates (Panel A) or PPP exchange rates (Panel B).

4. Based on recent average inflation rates of around 3 percent in WAEMU and 9 percent in non-WAEMU countries, one proposal under consideration is for the common central bank to target CPI inflation of 6 percent plus or minus 3 percent.

5. See Mohanty and Klau (2005) and the discussion in Anand, Prasad, and Zhang (2015).

CHAPTER 7

1. A conventional result, based on models in which price rigidities are the main friction, is that targeting core inflation is the optimal strategy for an inflation targeting central bank. Anand, Prasad, and Zhang (2015) show that, in models with credit constraints, targeting overall CPI improves welfare relative to core CPI targeting. Limited financial inclusion, which serves as one measure of household credit constraints, implies that this new result is highly relevant for emerging market and developing countries. This result is even stronger when one takes into account the high share of food expenditures in average household consumption expenditures in developing countries, particularly low-income ones (food prices are typically excluded from core CPI).

2. The need for harmonization of national statistics is relevant in other areas as well. For instance, not all ECOWAS countries seem to have fully and consistently adopted the IMF's Balance of Payments Manual 6 (BPM6) conventions for reporting balance of payments statistics.

3. There is no official definition of the eurozone "core." Adding Austria and Finland to the group, as some observers do, raises the core countries' share of eurozone GDP and population to 63 percent and 56 percent, respectively. GDP share calculations are based on 2017 nominal GDP.

4. A full official description of TARGET2 is available at the website "What Is TARGET2?" European Central Bank, www.ecb.europa.eu/explainers/tell-me/html /target2.en.html. The key elements, according to the ECB: TARGET2 is the real -time gross settlement (RTGS) system for the euro, where processing and settlement takes place in real time (that is, continuously) and each transfer is settled individually (gross settlement). Operated by the Eurosystem, TARGET2 enables transactions to be settled using central bank money and with immediate finality, and offers the highest standards of reliability and resilience. . . . The payments settled via TARGET2 relate mainly to refinancing operations with national central banks, transactions between credit institutions and settlement in central bank money conducted by other financial market infrastructures. . . . TARGET2 also plays a key role in ensuring the smooth transmission of monetary policy, the correct functioning of financial markets and banking, and financial stability in the euro area by substantially reducing systemic risk.

5. See Hans-Werner Zinn's October 2020 blog post "Target Balances" at www. hanswernersinn.de/en/topics/TargetBalances and Sinn and Wollmershäuser (2012).

6. The ECB paper summarizes its logic as follows: "The APP gives rise to sub-

stantial cross-border flows of reserves at the time of asset purchases and beyond, reflecting the interaction of decentralized monetary policy implementation and the integrated euro area financial structure. This financial structure, in which only a handful of locations act as gateways between the euro area and the rest of the world, leads to rising TARGET balances at the time of APP purchases and the persistence of TARGET balances in the context of subsequent portfolio rebalancing. TARGET balances per se are not necessarily an indicator of stress in bank funding markets, financial market fragmentation, or unsustainable balance of payments developments."

CHAPTER 8

1. Details about the ETLS can be found at www.etls.ecowas.int. A broader description of trade and market integration initiatives under the umbrella of ECOWAS is available at www.uneca.org/oria/pages/ecowas-trade-and-market-integration. One specific recent initiative is the West Africa trade facilitation program (see "ECOWAS Deliberates on West Africa Trade Facilitation Program," ECOWAS, September 30, 2018, www.ecowas.int/ecowas-deliberates-on-west-africa-trade -facilitation-programme).

APPENDIX A

1. The ASEAN-6 (Negara Brunei Darussalam, Indonesia, Malaysia, the Philippines, Singapore, and Thailand) have reduced 99 percent of tariff lines in the Inclusion List to zero percent import duty; Cambodia, Laos, Myanmar, Vietnam reduced 91 percent of tariff lines in the list to zero import duty.

2. [46] Rules of Origin with minimum local value content requirement of 45 percent f.o.b. (35 percent for LDCs).

3. The eleven EMEAP central banks are Reserve Bank of Australia, the People's Bank of China, Hong Kong Monetary Authority, Bank Indonesia, Bank of Japan, Bank of Korea, Bank Negara Malaysia, Reserve Bank of New Zealand, Bangko Sentral ng Pilipinas, Monetary Authority of Singapore, and Bank of Thailand.

4. The nine AFB2 Funds include a Pan-Asian Bond Index Fund (PAIF) and eight single-market bond index funds (China, Hong Kong, Indonesia, Korea, Malaysia, Philippines, Singapore, and Thailand).

5. European Union, "European Central Bank," https://europa.eu/european -union/about-eu/institutions-bodies/european-central-bank_en.

6. European Central Bank, "Decisionmaking," http://www.ecb.europa.eu/ecb/ orga/decisions/govc/html/index.en.html.

7. European Commission, "Role of the European Commission," https://ec. europa.eu/info/role-european-commission_en.

8. Eurostat, "Who Does What," http://ec.europa.eu/eurostat/about/overview/ who-does-what.

9. European Central Bank, "European System of Financial Supervision," www .bankingsupervision.europa.eu/about/esfs/html/index.en.html.

10. European Central Bank, "What Is TARGET2," www.ecb.europa.eu/ explainers/tell-me/html/target2.en.html.

11. The benchmark for a severe economic downturn is now a negative annual

real GDP growth rate or an accumulated loss of output during a protracted period of very low annual real GDP growth relative to potential growth.

12. Regarding the medium-term economic position, these include, in particular, potential growth, the prevailing cyclical conditions, the implementation of the Lisbon Agenda, and policies to foster research and development and innovation. Relevant developments in the medium-term budgetary position include fiscal consolidation efforts in "good times," debt sustainability, public investment, and the overall quality of public finances. Consideration should also be given to any other factors which, in the opinion of the member state concerned, are relevant to a comprehensive assessment of the excess over the reference value in qualitative terms. Special consideration will be given to budgetary efforts toward increasing or maintaining a high level of financial contributions with the aim of fostering international solidarity and achieving European policy goals, notably the unification of Europe, if they have a detrimental effect on the growth and fiscal burden of the member state.

13. The standard deadline for correcting an excessive deficit remains the "year following its identification unless there are special circumstances." However, the consideration of whether there are special circumstances justifying an extension by one year should take into account a balanced overall assessment of the "other relevant factors" mentioned above.

APPENDIX B

1. IMF, "West African Economic and Monetary Union," April 2017, www.imf.org/en/Publications/CR/Issues/2017/04/26/West-African-Economic-and-Monetary-Union-Common-Policies-of-Member-Countries-Press-Release-44867.

2. IMF, "Central African Economic and Monetary Community," September 2016, https://www.imf.org/external/pubs/ft/scr/2016/cr16290.pdf.

3. The basic fiscal balance is defined as total revenue (net of grants) minus total expenditure, excluding foreign-financed capital spending. It is measured at the central government level.

4. The calculation formula has been revised to consider oil revenues. Overall balance with an oil revenues savings rule = (Overall balance)/GDP – α(oil revenues)/GDP. The parameter α represents the share of oil revenues to be saved by each country, based on three-year (country-specific) averages to smooth out short-term fluctuations.

5. European Union, "Convergence Criteria for Joining," https://ec.europa.eu/info/business-economy-euro/euro-area/enlargement-euro-area/convergence-criteria-joining_en. European Central Bank, "Fiscal Policies," www.ecb.europa.eu/mopo/eaec/fiscal/html/index.en.html. European Commission, "Stepping Up or Abrogating the EDP," https://ec.europa.eu/info/business-economy-euro/economic-and-fiscal-policy-coordination/eu-economic-governance-monitoring-prevention-correction/stability-and-growth-pact/corrective-arm-excessive-deficit-procedure/stepping-or-abrogating-edp_en.

6. The SADC is not a currency union, but the CMA is inside the SADC. SADC also wants to expand the model of CMA to the whole community. SADC, "Regional

Indicative Strategic Development Plan," SADC, March 2001, www.sadc.int/files/5713/5292/8372/Regional_Indicative_Strategic_Development_Plan.pdf.

7. IMF, "East Caribbean Currency Union: Selected Issues," June 2017, www.imf.org/~/media/Files/Publications/CR/2017/cr17151.ashx.

APPENDIX C

1. The analysis in this section is based largely on work done by Tilahun Emiru.

2. This approach makes it easier to generalize the model to study intermediate exchange rate regimes. Technically, it is not the same as a fixed exchange rate since, in that case, the domestic interest rate would be pinned down by the world interest rate and interest parity conditions. Substantively, the differences in results are minor.

3. For instance, Broda and Tille (2003) conclude that "Sharp swings in a developing country's terms of trade—the price of its exports relative to the price of its imports—can seriously disrupt output growth. An analysis of the effects of a decline in export prices in seventy-five developing economies suggests that countries with a flexible exchange rate will experience a much milder contraction in output than their counterparts with fixed exchange rate regimes."

BIBLIOGRAPHY

Adam, Anokye M., and Imran Sharif Chaudhry (2014). "The Currency Union Effect on Intra-Regional Trade in Economic Community of West African States (ECOWAS)." *Journal of International Trade Law and Policy* 13, No. 2, pp. 102–22.

Afrika, Jean-Guy K., and Gerald Ajumbo (2012). "Informal Cross Border Trade in Africa: Implications and Policy Recommendations." *Africa Economic Brief* 3, No. 10, African Development Bank.

Aghion, Philippe, Philippe Bacchetta, Romain Rancière, and Kenneth Rogoff (2009). "Exchange Rate Volatility and Productivity Growth: The Role of Financial Development." *Journal of Monetary Economics* 56, No. 4, pp. 494–513.

Aizenman, Joshua, Menzie Chinn, and Hiro Ito (2010). "The Emerging Global Financial Architecture: Tracing and Evaluating New Patterns of the Trilemma Configuration." *Journal of International Money and Finance* 29, No. 4, pp. 615–41.

Aizenman, Joshua, Menzie Chinn, and Hiro Ito (2011). "Surfing the Waves of Globalization: Asia and Financial Globalization in the Context of the Trilemma." *Journal of the Japanese and International Economies* 25, No. 3, pp. 290–320.

Alagidede, Paul, Simeon Coleman, and Juan Carlos Cuestas (2012). "Inflationary Shocks and Common Economic Trends: Implications for West African Monetary Union Membership." *Journal of Policy Modeling* 34, No. 3, pp. 460–75.

Anand, Rahul, Eswar S. Prasad, and Boyang Zhang (2015). "What Measure of Inflation Should a Developing Country Central Bank Target?" *Journal of Monetary Economics* 74, pp. 102–16.

Asongu, Simplice, Jacinta Nwachukwu, and Vanessa Tchamyou (2017). "A Literature Survey on Proposed African Monetary Unions." *Journal of Economic Surveys* 31, No. 3, pp. 878–902.

Bahmani-Oskooee, M., S. Hegerty, and A. Kutan (2008). "Do Nominal Devaluations Lead to Real Devaluations? Evidence from 89 Countries." *International Review of Economics and Finance* 17, pp. 644–70.

Bakoup, Ferdinand, and Daniel Ndoye (2016). "Why and When to Introduce a Single Currency in ECOWAS." Chief Africa Economic Brief 7, No. 1, African Development Bank.

Baldwin, Richard E. (2006). "The Euro's Trade Effects." ECB Working Paper No. 594.

Barro, Robert, and David Gordon (1983). "A Positive Theory of Monetary Policy in a Natural Rate Model." *Journal of Political Economy* 91, No. 4, pp. 589–610.

Bayoumi, Tamim, and Barry Eichengreen (1994). "One Money or Many? Analyzing the Prospects for Monetary Unification in Various Parts of the World." *Studies in International Finance* 76. Princeton University Press.

Bayoumi, Tamim, and Eswar Prasad (1997). "Currency Unions, Economic Fluctuations and Adjustment: Some Empirical Evidence." *IMF Staff Papers* 44, No. 1, pp. 36–57.

Berg, Andrew, Carlos Goncalves, and Rafael Portillo (2018). "How Do Floating Exchange Rates Attenuate the Cycle?" *International Monetary Fund.*

Berg, Andrew, Stephen O'Connell, Catherine Pattillo, Rafael Portillo, and Filiz Unsal (2015). "Monetary Policy Issues in Sub-Saharan Africa." In *The Oxford Handbook of Africa and Economics: Volume 2: Policies and Practices*, edited by Célestin Monga and Justin Yifu Lin. Oxford University Press.

Boz, Emine, Gita Gopinath, and Mikkel Plagborg-Møller (2017). "Global Trade and the Dollar." NBER Working Paper No. 23988.

Broda, Christian (2004). "Terms of Trade and Exchange Rate Regimes in Developing Countries." *Journal of International Economics* 63, No. 1, pp. 31–58.

Broda, Christian M., and Cedric Tille (2003). "Coping with Terms-of-Trade Shocks in Developing Countries." *Current Issues in Economics and Finance* 9, No. 11.

Buiter, Willem, Giancarlo Corsetti, and Nouriel Roubini (1993). "Excessive Deficits: Sense and Nonsense in the Treaty of Maastricht." *Economic Policy* 8, No. 16, pp. 57–100.

Bun, Maurice J. G., Franc Klaassen, and Randolph Tan (2009). "Free Trade Areas and Intra-Regional Trade: The Case of ASEAN." *Singapore Economic Review* 54, No. 3, pp. 319–34.

Calderón, César, Alberto Chong, and Ernesto Stein (2007). "Trade Intensity and Business Cycle Synchronization: Are Developing Countries any Different?" *Journal of International Economics* 71, No. 1, pp. 2–21.

Calvo, Guillermo, and Carmen Reinhart (2002). "Fear of Floating." *Quarterly Journal of Economics* 107, pp. 379–408.

Calvo, Guillermo, and Carlos Vegh (1994). "Inflation Stabilization and Nominal Anchors." *Contemporary Economic Policy* 12, pp. 35–45.

Canova, Fabio, and Matteo Ciccarelli (2013). "Panel Vector Autoregressive Models: A Survey." In *VAR Models in Macroeconomics—New Developments and Appli-*

cations: Essays in Honor of Christopher A. Sims, pp. 205–46. Bingley, UK: Emerald Group Publishing Limited.

Cashin, Paul, Luis F. Céspedes, and Ratna Sahay (2004). "Commodity Currencies and the Real Exchange Rate." *Journal of Development Economics* 75, No. 1, pp. 239–68.

Cashin, Paul, C. John McDermott, and Catherine Pattillo (2004). "Terms of Trade Shocks in Africa: Are They Short-Lived or Long-Lived?" *Journal of Development Economics* 73, No. 2, pp. 727–44.

Céspedes, Luis Felipe, and Andrés Velasco (2012). "Macroeconomic Performance during Commodity Price Booms and Busts." *IMF Economic Review* 60, No. 4, pp. 570–99.

Chan, Eric, Frank Packer, Eli M. Remolona, and Michael Chui (2011). "Local Currency Bond Markets and the Asian Bond Fund 2 Initiative." BIS Paper No. 63, pp. 35–61.

Chen, Yu-chin, and Kenneth Rogoff (2003). "Commodity Currencies." *Journal of International Economics* 60, No. 1, pp. 133–60.

Clarida, Richard H., Jordi Gali, and Mark Gertler (1999). "The Science of Monetary Policy: A New Keynesian Perspective." *Journal of Economic Literature* 37, No. 4, pp. 1661–1707.

Corden, W. Maxwell (1972). "Monetary Integration, Essays in International Finance." *International Finance Section*, No. 93, Princeton University, Department of Economics.

Cossé, Stéphane, Johannes Mueller, Jean Le Dem, and Jean A. P. Clément (1996). "Aftermath of the CFA Franc Devaluation." IMF Occasional Papers No. 138.

Couharde, Cécile, Issiaka Coulibaly, David Guerreiro, and Valérie Mignon (2013). "Revisiting the Theory of Optimum Currency Areas: Is the CFA Franc Zone Sustainable?" *Journal of Macroeconomics* 38, pp. 428–41.

Coulibaly, Brahima (2009). "Currency Unions and Currency Crises: An Empirical Assessment." *International Journal of Finance and Economics* 14, No. 3, pp. 199–221.

Coulibaly, Issiaka, and Blaise Gnimassoun (2013). "Optimality of a Monetary Union: New Evidence from Exchange Rate Misalignments in West Africa." *Economic Modelling* 32, pp. 463–82.

Dagher, Jihad, Jan Gottschalk, and Rafael Portillo (2012). "The Short-Run Impact of Oil Windfalls in Low-Income Countries: A DSGE Approach." *Journal of African Economies* 21, No. 3, pp. 343–72.

Daude, Christian, Eduardo Levy-Yeyati, and Arne Nagengast (2016). "On the Effectiveness of Exchange Rate Interventions in Emerging Markets." *Journal of International Money and Finance*, 64, No. C, pp. 239–61.

De Grauwe, Paul (2000). *Economics of Monetary Union*. Oxford University Press.

Deaton, Angus, and Ron Miller (1996). "International Commodity Prices, Macroeconomic Performance and Politics in Sub-Saharan Africa." *Journal of African Economies* 5, No. 3, pp. 99–191.

Debrun, Xavier, Paul Masson, and Catherine Pattillo (2003). "West African Currency Unions: Rationale and Sustainability." *CESifo Economic Studies* 49, No. 3, pp. 381–413.

Debrun, Xavier, Paul Masson, and Catherine Pattillo (2005). "Monetary Union in West Africa: Who Might Gain, Who Might Lose, and Why?" *Canadian Journal of Economics* 38, No. 2, pp. 454–81.

Debrun, Xavier, Paul Masson, and Catherine Pattillo (2010). "Should African Monetary Unions Be Expanded? An Empirical Investigation of the Scope for Monetary Integration in Sub-Saharan Africa." IMF Working Paper No. 10/157.

Devarajan, Santayana, and Lawrence E. Hinkle (1994). "The CFA Franc Parity Change: An Opportunity to Restore Growth and Reduce Poverty." *Africa Spectrum* 29, No. 2, pp. 131–51.

Devarajan, Shantayanan, and Dani Rodrik (1991). "Do the Benefits of Fixed Exchange Rates Outweigh Their Costs? The CFA Zone in Africa." In *Open Economies: Structural Adjustment and Agriculture*, edited by Ian Goldin and L. Alan Winters. Cambridge University Press.

Devereux, Michael B., Philip R. Lane, and Juanyi Xu (2006). "Exchange Rates and Monetary Policy in Emerging Market Economies." *Economic Journal* 116, No. 511, pp. 478–506.

Di Giovanni, Julian, and Jay Shambaugh (2008). "The Impact of Foreign Interest Rates on the Economy: The Role of the Exchange Rate Regime." *Journal of International Economics* 74, No. 2, pp. 341–61.

Diop, Samba, Peter Tillmann, and Peter Winker (2017). "A Monetary Stress Indicator for the Economic Community of West African States." *Journal of African Development* 19, No. 2, pp. 1–18.

Dupasquier, Chantal, Patrick N. Osakwe, and Shandre M. Thangavelu (2005). "Choice of Monetary and Exchange Regimes in ECOWAS: An Optimum Currency Area Analysis." Working Paper No. 22570. East Asian Bureau of Economic Research.

Ebi, Ernest (2003). "Regional Currency Areas: Lessons from the West African Subregion and Nigeria's Policy Stance." *Currency Areas and the Use of Foreign Currencies* 17, pp. 145–50. Bank of International Settlements.

ECOWAS (2000). "Accra Declaration on Creation of a Second Monetary Zone."

Edwards, Sebastian, and Eduardo Levy Yeyati (2005). "Flexible Exchange Rates as Shock Absorbers." *European Economic Review* 49, No. 8, pp. 2079–3005.

Eichengreen, Barry (1992). "Is Europe an Optimum Currency Area?" In *The European Community after 1992: Perspectives from the Outside,* edited by Silvio Borner and Herbert Grubel. London: Macmillan.

Eisenschmidt, Jens, Danielle Kedan, Martin Schmitz, Ramón Adalid, and Patrick Papsdorf (2017). "The Eurosystem's Asset Purchase Program and TARGET Balances." ECB Occasional Paper No. 196.

Elliott, Robert J. R., and Kengo Ikemoto (2004). "AFTA and the Asian Crisis: Help or Hindrance to ASEAN Intra-Regional Trade?" *Asian Economic Journal* 18, No. 1, pp. 1–23.

Fielding, David, Kevin Lee, and Kalvinder Shields (2011). "Does One Size Fit All? Modeling Macroeconomic Linkages in the West African Economic and Monetary Union." *Economic Change and Restructuring* 45, No. 1–2, pp. 45–70.

Fischer, Stanley (2001). "Exchange Rate Regimes: Is the Bipolar View Correct?" *Journal of Economic Perspectives* 15, No. 2, pp. 3–24.

Frankel, Jeffrey (1999). "No Single Exchange Rate Regime Is Right for All Countries or at All Times." *Essays in International Finance*, No. 215. Princeton University Press.

Frankel, Jeffrey (2005). "Contractionary Currency Crashes in Developing Countries." *IMF Staff Papers* 52, No. 2, pp. 149–92.

Frankel, Jeffrey (2007). "On the Rand: Determinants of the South African Exchange Rate." *South African Journal of Economics* 75, No. 3, pp. 425–41.

Frankel, Jeffrey (2010). "The Estimated Effects of the Euro on Trade: Why Are They Below Historical Effects of Monetary Unions Among Smaller Countries?" In *Europe and the Euro*, edited by Alberto Alesina and Francesco Giavazzi, pp. 169–218. University of Chicago Press.

Frankel, Jeffrey (2011). "Are Bilateral Remittances Countercyclical?" *Open Economies Review* 22, No. 1, pp. 1–16.

Frankel, Jeffrey A. (2012). "Choosing an Exchange Rate Regime." In *Handbook of Exchange Rates*, edited by Jessica James, Ian W. Marsh, and Lucio Sarno, pp. 765–83, Hoboken, NJ: Wiley.

Frankel, Jeffrey A., and Andrew K. Rose (1998). "The Endogeneity of the Optimum Currency Area Criteria." *Economic Journal* 108, No. 449, pp. 1009–25.

Frankel, Jeffrey A., and Andrew K. Rose (2002). "An Estimate of the Effect of Common Currencies on Trade and Income." *Quarterly Journal of Economics* 117, No. 2, pp. 437–66.

Frieden, Jeffry (2014). "Currency Politics: The Political Economy of Exchange Rate Policy." Princeton University Press.

Friedman, Milton (1953). "The Case for Flexible Exchange Rates." In M. Friedman, *Essays in Positive Economics*, pp. 157–203. University of Chicago Press.

Gilbert, John, Robert Scollay, and Bijit Bora (2001). "Assessing Regional Trading Arrangements in the Asia-Pacific." *UN Policy Issues in International Trade and Commodities Study Series* No. 15.

Glick, Reuven, and Andrew Rose (2002). "Does a Currency Union Affect Trade? The Time Series Evidence." *European Economic Review* 46, pp. 1125–51.

Gopinath, Gita, Emine Boz, Camila Casas, Federico J. Díez, Pierre-Olivier Gourinchas, and Mikkel Plagborg-Møller (2020). "Dominant Currency Paradigm." *American Economic Review* 110, No. 3, pp. 677–719.

Goncalves, Carlos (2015). "Taylor Visits Africa." IMF Working Paper No. 15/258.

Goswami, Mangal, and Sunil Sharma (2011). "The Development of Local Debt Markets in Asia." IMF Working Paper No. 11/132.

Harvey, Simon K., and Matthew J. Cushing (2015). "Is West African Monetary Zone (WAMZ) a Common Currency Area?" *Review of Development Finance* 5, No. 1, pp. 53–63.

Hoffmaister, Alexander W., and Jorge E. Roldos (2001). "The Sources of Macroeconomic Fluctuations in Developing Countries: Brazil and Korea." *Journal of Macroeconomics* 23, No. 2, pp. 213–39.

Holtz-Eakin, Douglas, Whitney Newey, and Harvey S. Rosen (1988). "Estimating Vector Autoregressions with Panel Data." *Econometrica* 56, No. 6, pp. 1371–95.

Honohan, Patrick, and Philip R. Lane (2001). "Will the Euro Trigger More Monetary Unions in Africa?" In *The Impact of EMU on Europe and the Developing Countries*, edited by Charles Wyplosz, pp. 315–38. Oxford University Press.

Houssa, Romain (2008). "Monetary Union in West Africa and Asymmetric Shocks: A Dynamic Structural Factor Model Approach." *Journal of Development Economics* 85, No. 1, pp. 319–47.

Huchet, Marilyne (2003). "Does Single Monetary Policy Have Asymmetric Real Effects in EMU?" *Journal of Policy Modeling* 25, No. 2, pp. 151–78.

IMF (2014). "Long-Run Growth and Macroeconomic Stability in Low-Income Countries—The Role of Structural Transformation and Diversification." IMF Policy Papers.

IMF (2015). "West African Economic and Monetary Community: Selected Issues." IMF Country Report No. 15/101.

IMF (2016). "Central African Economic and Monetary Community: Selected Issues." IMF Country Report No. 16/290.

IMF (2017). "Regional Economic Outlook: Fiscal Adjustment and Economic Diversification." IMF Regional Economic Outlook: Sub-Saharan Africa.

IMF (2018). "IMF Executive Board Discusses Program Design in Currency Unions." IMF Press Release No. 18/90.

Itakura, Ken (2014). "Impact of Liberalization and Improved Connectivity and Facilitation in ASEAN." *Journal of Asian Economics* 35, pp. 2–11.

Ji, Xianbai, Pradumna Bickram Rana, Chia Wai Mun, and Changtai Li (2018). "Trade Policy Options for ASEAN Countries and Their Regional Dialogue Partners: 'Preference Ordering' Using CGE Analysis." RSiS Working Paper No. 308.

Jugurnath, Bhavish, Mark Stewart, and Robert Brooks (2007). "Asia/Pacific Regional Trade Agreements: An Empirical Study." *Journal of Asian Economics* 18, pp. 974–87.

Kenen, Peter (1969). "The Theory of Optimum Currency Areas: An Eclectic View." In *Monetary Problems in the International Economy*, pp. 41–60. University of Chicago Press.

Kitwiwattanachai, Anyarath, Doug Nelson, Geoffrey Reed (2010). "Quantitative Impacts of Alternative East Asia Free Trade Areas: A Computable General Equilibrium (CGE) Assessment." *Journal of Policy Modeling* 32, No. 2, pp. 286–301.

Kuteesa, Annette (2012). "East African Regional Integration: Challenges in Meeting the Convergence Criteria for Monetary Union: A Survey." *International Journal of Economics and Finance* 4, No. 10.

Levy-Yeyati, Eduardo, and Federico Sturzenegger (2003). "To Float or to Fix: Evidence on the Impact of Exchange Rate Regimes." *American Economic Review* 93, No. 4, pp. 1173–93.

Maliszewska, Maryla, Zoryana Olekseyuk, and Israel Osorio-Rodarte (2018). "Economic and Distributional Impacts of Comprehensive and Progressive Agreement for Trans-Pacific Partnership: The Case of Vietnam." World Bank Group Report.

Mansoor, Ali, Salifou Issoufou, and Daouda Sembene (2018). "The Sustainability of Senegal's Public Debt." In *Race to the Next Income Frontier: How Senegal and Other Low-Income Countries Can Reach the Finish Line*. International Monetary Fund.

Masson, Paul R., Catherine Pattillo, and Xavier Debrun (2015). "The Future of African Monetary Geography." In *The Oxford Handbook of Africa and Economics,*

Volume 2: Policies and Practices, edited by Célestin Monga and Justin Yifu Lin. Oxford University Press.

McKinnon, Ronald I. (1963). "Optimum Currency Areas." *American Economic Review* 53, No. 4, pp. 717–25.

Mendoza, Enrique G. (1995). "The Terms of Trade, the Real Exchange Rate, and Economic Fluctuations." *International Economic Review* 36, No. 1, pp. 101–37.

Mensah, Isaac (2015). "Monetary and Economic Union in West Africa: An Analysis on Trade." *International Journal of Business and Economic Sciences Applied Research* 8, No. 2, pp. 87–118.

Mishkin, Frederic S. (2000). "Inflation Targeting in Emerging-Market Countries." *American Economic Review* 90, No. 2, pp. 105–09.

Mody, Ashoka (2018). *Euro Tragedy: A Drama in Nine Acts*. Princeton University Press.

Mohanty, Madhusudan S., and Marc Klau (2005). "Monetary Policy Rules in Emerging Market Economies: Issues and Evidence." In *Monetary Policy and Macroeconomic Stabilization in Latin America*, pp. 205–45. Edited by Rolf J. Langhammer and Lúcio Vinhas de Souza. Springer Science & Business Media.

Monga, Célestin (2015). "African Monetary Unions: An Obituary." In *The Oxford Handbook of Africa and Economics, Volume 2: Policies and Practices*, edited by Célestin Monga and Justin Yifu Lin. Oxford University Press.

Mundell, Robert A. (1961). "A Theory of Optimum Currency Areas." *American Economic Review* 51, No. 4, pp. 657–65.

Mundell, Robert A. (1976). "The Choice of Monetary Systems: African Currency Problems." In *Africa and Monetary Integration*, edited by Rodrigue Tremblay, pp. 363–68. Montreal: Les Editions HRW.

Ndulu, Benno, and Joseph Leina Masawe (2015). "Challenges of Central Banking in Africa." In *The Oxford Handbook of Africa and Economics, Volume 2: Policies and Practices*, edited by Célestin Monga and Justin Yifu Lin. Oxford University Press.

Nubukpo, Kako Kossivi (2017). "Misalignment of Exchange Rates: What Lessons for Growth and Policy Mix in the WAEMU?" Global Economic Governance Working Paper No. 126.

Obstfeld, Maurice, and Kenneth S. Rogoff (1995). "The Mirage of Fixed Exchange Rates." *Journal of Economic Perspectives* 9, No. 4, pp. 73–96.

Pesaran, M. Hashem (2015). *Time Series and Panel Data Econometrics*. Oxford University Press.

Pesaran, M. Hashem, Til Schuermann, and Scott M. Weiner (2004). "Modeling Regional Interdependencies Using a Global Error-Correcting Macroeconometric Model." *Journal of Business & Economic Statistics* 22, No. 2, pp. 129–62.

Prasad, Eswar S. (2014). "Distributional Effects of Macroeconomic Policy Choices in Emerging Market Economies." *IMF Economic Review* 62, No. 3, pp. 409–29.

Prasad, Eswar (2019). "ECOWAS Currency Union: Options and Considerations." Manuscript, Cornell University and Brookings Institution.

Prasad, Eswar, and Boyang Zhang (2015). "Distributional Effects of Monetary Policy in Emerging Market Economies." NBER Working Paper No. 21471.

Quah, Chee-Heong (2016). "A Diagnostic on the West African Monetary Union." *South African Journal of Economics* 84, No. 1, pp. 129–48.

Reinhart, Carmen M., and Kenneth S. Rogoff (2004). "The Modern History of Exchange Rate Arrangements: A Reinterpretation." *Quarterly Journal of Economics* 119, No. 1, pp. 1–48.

Saka, Jimoh Olakunle, Ibiyemi Ajoke Onafowokan, and Adekunle Ademayowa Adebayo (2015). "Analysis of Convergence Criteria in a Proposed Monetary Union: A Study of the Economic Community of West African States." *International Journal of Economics and Financial Issues* 5, No. 1, pp. 230–39.

Schmitt-Grohé, Stephanie, and Martín Uribe (2018). "How Important are Terms-of-Trade Shocks?" *International Economic Review* 59, No. 1, pp. 85–111.

Sinn, Hans-Werner, and Timo Wollmershäuser (2012). "Target Loans, Current Account Balances, and Capital Flows: The ECB's Rescue Facility." *International Tax and Public Finance* 19, No. 4, pp. 468–508.

Siri, Alain (2012). "Monetary Policy Rules: Lessons Learned from ECOWAS Countries." AERC Research Paper No. 244.

Tchatchouang, Jean-Claude (2015). "The CFA Franc Zone: A Biography." In *The Oxford Handbook of Africa and Economics, Volume 2: Policies and Practices*, edited by Célestin Monga and Justin Yifu Lin. Oxford University Press.

Tsangarides, Charalambos G., and Mahvash Saeed Qureshi (2008). "Monetary Union Membership in West Africa: A Cluster Analysis." *World Development* 36, No. 7, pp. 1261–79.

USAID (2015). "EADS Analytical Brief on Trade in West Africa." EADS Analytical Brief, No. 1, USAID.

Usman, Abdullateef, and Waheed Ibrahim (2012). "Foreign Direct Investment and Monetary Union in ECOWAS Subregion: Lessons from Abroad." *Journal of Applied Finance and Banking* 2, No. 4, pp. 185–92.

Vithessonthi, Chaiporn, and Sriyalatha Kumarasinghe (2016). "Financial Development, International Trade Integration, and Stock Market Integration: Evidence from Asia." *Journal of Multinational Financial Management* 35, pp. 79–92.

Yang, Shanping, and Inmaculada Martinez-Zarzoso (2014). "A Panel Data Analysis of Trade Creation and Trade Diversion Effects: The Case of ASEAN–China Free Trade Area." *China Economic Review* 29, pp. 138–51.

Zhao, Xiaodan, and Yoonbai Kim (2009). "Is the CFA Franc Zone an Optimum Currency Area?" *World Development* 37, No. 12, pp. 1877–86.

INDEX